Turned Wrong at Ding Dong

Texas, Travels and Opinions on Everything

By Adrian Jackson

Nothing says Texas like a drive-thru liquor barn. If you've ever driven through one you know it is floor to ceiling liquor. It is like a museum. It's an awe inspiring collection of scotch, beer, whiskey, brown liquor, blue liquor, creamy white liquor, hard stuff, girly stuff, and mixed drinks. The bartender came to my car with a tray full of Styrofoam cups. Each had a sliver of clear tape across the straw hole. I thought, *Is he kidding? A piece of tape?* That slight piece of tape was apparently going to save my ass from jail, should I have gotten pulled over by the police.

Adrian Jackson is a freelance columnist in Beeville, Texas. She holds a master's degree from Texas Tech University (Go Red Raiders!). In her spare time, she works at a local college; raises a daughter, a pair of Labs, and a cat; and entertains the idea of earning a Ph.D.

Introduction 8

Drive-thru drinks 12

Taking the scenic route to Centex 13

Ike never made it to Beeville 15

Texas mystery remains unsolved 17

Happy St. Patrick's Day, ya'll! 19

Headed to Spring Ho 20

My spirit soared 22

Kids can learn a lot from the symphony 24

Where's the #@*%$!!! border? 26

Hoping and praying for rain 28

Is there a Yellow Rose? 30

Looking forward to traveling the Coastal Bend 32

Remembering Lady Bird 34

Becoming a Texan (a lifetime to go….) 36

Lessons learned while lost in the woods 37

Those weirdo livestock kids 39

Goodbye, Little Red 40

Here's how the visit went 42

Time for our last hurrah 44

A new kind of flower grows in West Texas 46

Oh! The places you'll go 48

I think I see Mickey 49

I ♥ TEXAS 50

Forget Paris	51
Airport lounge visit yields more than free snacks	53
Greetings from the airport	55
Body search is too personal	57
Give me a 'chute; keep your floatie	59
Watching people to pass the time	60
A privilege for whom?	62
New Jersey is where the heart is	64
My cup runneth over	66
School kids face serious dangers	68
You'll get blind trust from me	69
How much is too much?	70
The death of a servicemember	71
Ear worms are taking over the world	73
It's summer. How're your feet?	74
Be careful who your friends are	76
Dear Future Me,	78
Albums that changed my life	79
Great Books I	82
Great Books II	84
How far would I go for Turkish Delight?	85
Mean Girls	87
Fashion faux pas	89
What's up with Smilin' Bob?	90

How old is too old to drive? I don't know 92

A look into past lives 93

Is she or isn't she? 94

A boy named Sassy 95

My cat sneaks out the back door 96

Science and math for girls 98

Fit is fine, but skinny is scary 100

My take on spankings 102

Get to know me for me 104

Shopping at 5 a.m. 105

Great gifts for holiday shoppers 107

The best and the worst gifts 108

Card games make handy stocking stuffers 110

Christmastime is here 112

A cancer walk for Summer 114

Happy 106th Summer Jean 116

$5 for a toothbrush? 118

Tooth Fairy 119

Dogs, trucks and bad things that happen 120

Be wary of strangers at the door 121

Remembering the victim 123

Toddler dies by the hands of a monster 125

I occupied a black space 127

Existing in a virtual reality 129

Can you pass a citizenship test?..131

So you want to be a U.S. citizen?......................................133

Is that moron your cousin?..135

Doogie Houser, M.D..137

The end is nigh..139

10 things to do before I die...141

Dying with Dignity...142

What I want in a president 144

Name-calling hurts..146

We can all get along..148

Go vote..150

Change is coming; We are moving on up 152

Great-grandmother leaves a lasting legacy......................154

Census reveals forgotten details about family tree.........156

Reality TV does nothing for me...158

Congratulations, graduates …. what's next for you?........160

20 years out of high school...162

Mrs. Jones is a lady on Hudson Street 164

I won't pass poverty on to my daughter..........................166

My life in decades...168

How does my garden grow?...170

Young life lost to shot to the head....................................172

Reporters mishandle a tragic story...................................174

Ya want keffiyeh with that doughnut?.............................176

What's wrong with the Suleman 8? 178

Bertinelli is not your typical cover model 180

Take a hike, Heloise! 182

I am a filing disaster 184

It ain't easy going green 186

I'm still green 188

If Longoria uses reusable bags, you should too 190

Author baffled by the change 192

One child is enough for me 194

A shy and awkward girl 196

Disney Movies 197

Least-loved child waits longest to be picked up 198

Don't give me a hand 200

Who is a hero? 202

Musicals are making a comeback 203

Death to the doppelganger 205

The other N word 206

Sept 11: Am I ready to be entertained? 207

Olympic hopeless gears up for summer games 209

The Oscar goes to... 211

Smell my pits, you freak! 213

Hollywood is beckoning me 214

Shopping cart rules 216

Teen pregnancy is not cool 218

Word	220
New Words	221
Environment on the minds of dictionary makers	223
The thrill is gone	225
Oh, how I love bacon	227
Forget Paris Hilton	228
I hate homework	229
Will I ever succeed in math?	231
Teens can succeed	233
What's in a name?	234
Soccer: A proving ground	235
the pitfalls of spelling & grandma	236
Life's like a box of Mockolates??!	238
Just say 'thank you'	240
It's time to make upgrades	241

Introduction

People ask me where I get ideas for my articles from. I get them from life. My life. My everyday life.

I don't think that I'm a particularly interesting person. I'm no more or less interesting than the next schlub. I go to work every day. I manage a household. I chauffer my kid around to 100 different activities a week. I try to eat right. I exercise on occasion. I love my mom. I feed my dog. I shake the gas pump handle before putting it back in its cradle.

But, I have a wry sense of humor, so I usually see things with a comical tint. That's a gift. If I weren't able to look at things, laugh and shrug, I think I'd be a bitter person. I feel sorry for people who don't see the humor of life.

I have the ability to look at a situation from different angles and accept the perspective that is easiest to live with. When things happen to me I think, 'Hmm. This is going to make a good article.' When a store clerk makes me angry, when I say the wrong thing or when I get mishandled at an airport, I look at it as an opportunity. I tell myself the story over and over until I've come up with just the right words to make it amusing. It all comes down to the telling.

I've got a gift for telling stories. I can spin a good yarn. I don't lie about my life but I've been known to stretch and bend a little for a laugh. My foibles make for good entertainment.

I think you have to laugh at yourself. It is a survival mechanism. I try not to take myself too seriously. I am as goofy, forgetful and dumb as I am intuitive, intelligent and philosophical, and I hope it all comes out in my work.

I try to be vague enough to illicit a response from the reader like, 'Hey. Something like that happened to me.' We are pack animals by nature and most of us have a simple need to empathize that is fed by stories we read, hear or see. I try to be specific enough to illicit a response from the reader like, 'I can't believe that happened to her.' As a writer, I want readers to be able to identify with me on some level. If I don't make a connection, I've failed. If I haven't already connected with you, be suspicious. This book may not be for you.

Sometimes, articles literally come to me. I overhear a conversation that makes me laugh or I engage in a discussion that reverberates in my head long after it has ended. I listen to sound bites. I tap into what 'everyone' is talking about. I recently chatted with someone about the dozens of naked Barbies located in my daughter's room. That article is just begging to be written.

But it's not all fun and games. Things happen that make me upset or angry and I use my column to speak out. Sometimes I speak on behalf of those who don't or can't speak for themselves like Elizabeth Campbell of Lampasas, Texas, who disappeared without a trace, and Elora McKemy, a two-year-old American who was raped and murdered and left in a gravel ditch in Babenhausen, Germany.

Injustice is a frequent topic of mine. It ranges from those who get in the wrong checkout lane to the –isms that force people to look at others differently.

There are rooms in my brain that I don't rummage through for materials. I don't write about my weight or my love life. There is no humor for me in these areas and I don't want to share. I don't write about my religion, faith or politics. These are polarizing issues. The field is overrun with columnists from these genres, so I'll leave this kind of writing to others.

There are boxes up in my mental attic that I won't open. I have many sad memories and terrible experiences from childhood. They are mine to keep. I don't want to share them anymore than you want to read them. So, I keep them taped up and stacked in the far corners of my mind.

The following pages are a record of my life. Compiling this book gave me the opportunity to reread things that I wrote years ago and share them with you. Since I'm not confined to the size of a newspaper column, I've extended many of these articles.

Topics covered run the gamut. Texas is frequently a theme since I am new to the state. I am always learning new things about Texas like what *caliche* is and why girls wear ribbons at the livestock show.

I write about my childhood in New Jersey and the decade I spent in Germany. I write about my family and friends and complete strangers who strike me as interesting. Sometimes I go off on a crazy tangent and write about things that only make sense to me. But through it all, I am cognizant of your presence and like any good hostess, I'm here to entertain.

Adrian Jackson is a freelance writer in Beeville, Texas. Her career and life have been made better with the love and support of the following: Abrianne Steele, LeAndrea Hilliard, Chrishele Luchey, Sandra Griggs, Carolyn Lewis, Geraldine Jackson, Thomas Steele, Family, Bee County friends and the Beeville Bee-Picayune staff.

TEXAS

Drive-thru drinks

Nothing says Texas like a drive-thru liquor barn.

When I visited in 1995, I found that you can buy alcohol without ever leaving your car. There is something to be said for the ingenuity of that. I've traveled a lot and I've never seen a similar setup (not that I go cruising for liquor).

I came upon my first liquor barn at the urging of a friend, who thought it would be fun to send me out for mixed drinks. She gave me driving directions and a list and told me not to remove the tape. Huh?

Off I went in search of booze. I found it easy enough and pulled up to the window. The clerk asked me what I wanted and I told him. I paid cash and was told to drive forward.

If you've ever driven through a liquor barn you know it is floor to ceiling liquor. It is almost like a museum. It's an awe inspiring collection of scotch, beer, whiskey, brown liquor, blue liquor, creamy white liquor, hard stuff, girly stuff, and mixed drinks.

The bartender came to my car with a tray full of Styrofoam cups. Each had a sliver of clear tape across the straw hole. I smiled, put the tray on the seat next to me and drove away.

I thought, *Is he kidding? A piece of tape?*

That slight piece of tape was apparently going to save my ass from jail, should I have gotten pulled over by the police. That tape was the difference between a sealed and an open container.

I wondered what would happen if one of the cups tipped over and popped open. What if I were in an accident and liquor splattered everywhere? How quickly could the tape seal become undone and get me into trouble?

I didn't like driving back to my friend's house with taped cups of mixed drinks. I was nervous. There was too much that could unravel this very delicate delivery system. Never the less, I made it back to my friend's house. It was a ridiculous experience and my friend got a great laugh at my expense.

Here's to all things uniquely Texan -- jackalopes, brisket and that Texas institution known as the liquor barn.

Taking the scenic route to Centex

After many years of driving from my home in Beeville, Texas to my sister's in Killeen, I've finally decided on my favorite route north. I usually start off either early morning or late evening. I try to time it so that I when I hit Austin, it is at a time when traffic is not awful, though truth be told, traffic is always pretty bad in Austin.

I've driven north in the middle of the night and still hit traffic jams at Ben White Boulevard. And if you get held up there you can forget about making it all the way to 38th Street in any reasonable amount of time. Some people slip off onto Mopac and bypass some of I-35. I've mastered Mopac driving south, having lived in Lampasas and used it to exchange from Highway 183, but I just can't make it work in the other direction. So, I avoid Austin as much as I can.

When I leave Beeville, I head up Highway 181 to Karnes City and then drive to U.S. 80. I used to hate this lonely highway, but I've found that muddling though Helena and Nixon (yawn) gets you to Luling and Lockhart, two beautiful little cities, stinky smell notwithstanding. Luling, where I move on to Highway 183, has a park that makes a great rest area if I need a break. Lockhart has a quickening of pace you usually find on the outskirts of a major city. By the time I hit the Caldwell-Travis County line, it's obvious that I've left rural Texas.

What makes this my new favorite route is the toll road just beyond Del Valle. For about $6 I can completely avoid Austin. The greatest thing about toll roads are the drivers who stay off of them. Local drivers don't use toll roads unless they are leaving town. Trucks don't use toll roads because they are not cost effective. Young drivers stay off of toll roads because they don't want to have to pay. That just leaves people like me – those of us who don't mind paying for some quiet and easy driving without congestion. I love toll roads. I could take Texas Toll Road 130 all the way to Georgetown, but I don't. I crossover to Texas Toll Road 45 and exit at Round Rock.

I love to stop at IKEA. No trip to Central Texas is complete without at least some window shopping at my favorite store. Visiting IKEA means getting on I-35 at Round Rock, and believe me, it's not as easy as Dell. That ten-mile strip between Round Rock and Georgetown can be as bad as Austin at times, but it is well worth it to make the side trip on the way.

At Georgetown, I slip on to Highway 195 toward Killeen. This is probably the most dangerous road in Texas. At some points it is a two-lane highway though it is the most popular route from Fort Hood to Austin's Sixth Street. Speeders and drunk drivers (I've actually seen people toss beer bottles out the car window) dominate this road after dark, so it is a prime location for some horrific accidents. Fortunately, truck traffic on this road is minimal. If it is late at night, I'll stay on I-35 to Belton and go west on Highway 190. If it is daytime, I'll drive west from Florence to Killeen where the only community in between is Ding Dong, Texas. The Bell County community is one of those blink-and-you'll-miss-it hamlets. I can't say for certain that I've actually driven through Ding Dong. The sign is there, but little else marks its location.

It's another lonely stretch of road that doesn't get interesting until the Central Texas State Veteran's Cemetery, located on a beautiful hilltop, comes into view.

Highway 195 takes me right to Fort Hood Street and on to my sister's house. The route is long and sometimes boring but I've made it my own. There is something to be said for the scenic route.

Adrian Jackson is a freelance writer in Beeville, Texas. She lived in Central Texas prior to moving south to Beeville.

Ike never made it to Beeville

Last week's hurricane was like a prom date. I spent days getting ready. I waited and waited. I opened the front door and looked up and down the street, but Ike was a no-show.

As a first time homebuyer, I was very nervous about this hurricane. I wasn't prepared and I didn't know how much work had to be done or what the cost would be. I actually didn't spend that much, having decided to forgo boarding up the windows. I sandbagged the doors thinking that at the very least we'd get a deluge.

I didn't realize that I would have to commit two days to hurricane preparedness. I did a lot of clean up outside and loaded the car with emergency essentials. These chores cost nothing but time. I took apart the trampoline, rearranged the garage, put the doghouse away and rounded up stray water hoses and garden tools. This project has actually helped improve the look of my property so it was time well spent though all for naught. Now I can say with confidence that I am more prepared for the next threat.

Unlike tornados, for which my only reference is the Kansas home that landed in Oz, I have some experience with hurricanes. I grew up in New Jersey and while hurricanes are not frequent, they happen. As a child, I remember having to run home from school one day ahead of a storm. My oldest sister was the last to arrive and literally jumped over uprooted trees to get home. That was the worst one, but there were plenty others.

We didn't evacuate in the 1970s. Technology wasn't as advanced as it is now. There was very little tracking of storms before they hit land. We just hunkered down as low to the floor as we could get and rode out the storm with our hands over our ears. Of course, I grew up in a three-story home with an attic and basement, so the threat of it being carried away by wind was pretty minimal though we occasionally got some basement flooding.

I recall the taping of windows, but I am unaware of what other hurricane preparations my family took. I remember my mother being terrified. She is afraid of thunderstorms and she scared the hell out of us when we were little. She made us unplug everything, avoid windows and if ever directly hit, the plan was to scamper into the claw-footed, cast iron bathtub.

With the expected arrival of Ike, I got some very solid advice from colleagues and relatives about what needed to be done. I rushed home on Wednesday to get my house ready.

We fully expected to evacuate on Thursday and though I hadn't finished the yard preparations, the car was road ready. Shortly after I got out of bed I realized that it would be completely unnecessary. The sky was clear and the weatherman was optimistic. Still, I was convinced that Ike would come.

By Friday, it was pretty clear that Bee County was not in any imminent danger but I expected that we would get some pretty nasty weather. We didn't, but I guess you already know that.

Saturday was surprisingly uneventful. I kept checking the sky expecting it to darken. When we went to the movies that evening, we heard the rumblings of a storm but it never arrived. Same thing Sunday. At that point it became obvious, even to me, that Ike was a no-show. I was relieved, though we sure could have used some of that rain.

My heart goes out to the people of Galveston, Houston, and Beaumont areas who are returning home to find that they have to start all over again. My thoughts and prayers go out to all of those who lost loved ones to the storm.

Texas mystery remains unsolved

Elizabeth Campbell disappeared on April 25, 1988. She was never heard from again.

I met Elizabeth's parents in 2004. They were old and sickly but still determined to find answers about what happened to their daughter the night she vanished. They dutifully put information about their daughter into the local papers every year in April, hoping that someone, somewhere would speak up about what happened to her. They want closure but to this day there are a myriad of questions and no answers.

Elizabeth, a college student in Killeen, was picked up after work by her boyfriend. They went to his house and had an argument. She called home to ask for a ride from her parents or siblings (two of whom were in Killeen at the same time that she was) but the boyfriend said he would drive her home to Lampasas, 30 miles away. She was angry with him and stormed out of the house. She somehow got a ride from Killeen to Copperas Cove (14 miles away), in the middle of the night. She stopped at the 7-11 in Copperas Cove to use a pay phone. A store clerk remembered her there.

And then, she was gone. No one knows if she left or was taken; if she was alone or with someone; or if she walked away or climbed into a car. No one knows what happened to Elizabeth after that moment.

Because she was 21 at the time, Elizabeth was never considered a missing child. It took a long fight to get a computer-simulated, age progression photo and registry on national missing persons lists. Her story aired on *Unsolved Mysteries* and if you search her name on the Internet, you'll see that her sister Barbara continues to search.

There were a few sightings reported but nothing that led to finding Elizabeth. Her parents drove from coast to coast looking for her, talking to experts and following leads. They made friends with unsavory characters who gave them small bits of information that ultimately led nowhere. The family turned in DNA samples so that the FBI would have a resource to use if ever a body turned up.

Four years after Elizabeth disappeared, her purse was found. It had been in the property room at the sheriff's department of a West Texas town that straddles I-10. The purse was the only concrete clue left behind and it was discovered too late to illicit any information that might have moved the case forward.

I met Elizabeth's parents Tom and Sam Soon Campbell on the anniversary of her disappearance. They invited me to their home to write an article about their daughter. They showed me decades of notes, business cards, and flyers. They showed me books that they'd written and photocopied to send to other parents of missing children on how to search and how to deal with law enforcement officials.

In some ways they were very bitter. Their daughter was robbed of a normal life. Their family was cheated by a fate that they can't even name. Was she abducted? Was she murdered? Did she run away? Is there anyone out there who knows what happened to Elizabeth?

When they lived in Lampasas they kept the porch light on just in case Elizabeth found her way home. Today, they are well into their 70s. Knowing that time is running out, they are still hoping for answers before they die. It is very possible that they will never get them.

Happy St. Patrick's Day, ya'll!

I'm from the East Coast and we know how to celebrate the patron saint of Ireland. It doesn't matter what your ethnicity, everybody's Irish on March 17. My family, New Jersey African-Americans that we are, never miss a celebration.

The coolest St. Patrick's Day I ever celebrated was in Dublin. I had a green shake at McDonald's and watched the Arkansas Razorback band perform in the grand parade. I tasted the bitter sting of a Guinness and shopped in Temple Bar.

I love to celebrate St. Patrick's Day. I brought that love to Texas and was delighted to discover that you can find corned beef at the local grocery store. Every year, I cook the beef with sides of cabbage and potatoes. I like to share this meal with friends. Few Texans have tasted a proper St. Patrick's Day feast like that.

One year, I inspired a friend so much that she went out on the very same day and bought some corned beef. She planned to cook it for her family as a special treat.

If you've never bought corned beef, it comes wrapped in plastic. It is covered in brine and there's a spice pack full of peppercorns stuck to it. If you don't know, brine is salt water and peppercorns season the meat (hence 'corned').

Even though corned beef is the same cut of beef as brisket, it is *not* brisket. My friend found this out when she failed to read the cooking instructions and popped the meat into the oven to roast. Naturally, the beef came out of the oven tender and juicy. I'm sure it looked very appealing and she couldn't wait to taste it. But, it was awful!

You've got to boil corned beef for about two hours before its edible. You've got to dump out the first pot of salty water and fill it up again. You've got to put the cabbage and potatoes in to absorb the rest of the salt. You've got to serve it with a good, strong mustard, not barbecue sauce.

My guess is that most Texans don't know how to cook corned beef. Only us transplants can do it right. I'm cooking corned beef this St. Patrick's Day. Who's coming to dinner?

Headed to Spring Ho

This weekend will mark the end of this year's *Spring Ho!*

Despite what you may assume, the annual Lampasas festival doesn't take place in spring and there isn't a harlot or garden tool to be found.

The week-long festival came about its name 35 years ago, when it was started. The word *Spring* comes from Lampasas' natural springs. When the railroad came to Lampasas it brought tourists from the North seeking the healing properties of its waters. Lampasas was billed, "The Saratoga of the South" and tourists came in droves.

Hancock Springs, just off of Highway 181, is the sight of the historic Hancock Bath House where visitors can see the largest spring gurgling from deep within the earth. In the same area, guests can take a dip in Hancock Park Free-Flow Swim Area, one of the last in the state to offer a refreshing dip in artesian (and by artesian I mean smelly) springs.

That explains *Spring*, but where in the world did the *Ho* come from? There are two possibilities:

Ho is short for hoedown. It was, after all, the 1970s when this name was adopted.

Ho is an expression of joy, as in *Land, Ho!* or *Westward, Ho!* or *Spring Ho!*

What started off as a weekend festival has grown to a week-long, citywide event with parades, a pageant, concerts, games, tournaments, and a carnival. County fair competitions are held during the week; the local museum celebrates with special exhibits; and several civic groups host related events. Lampasas High School reunions are held on the fives, so grads know when to come back and they do in large numbers.

Lampasas takes a lot of ribbing for the name of its festival. Jay Leno joked about it on the Tonight Show.

You can't imagine the abuse Miss Spring Ho and her court go through when they represent Lampasas throughout the state. Yet, every July the popular festival rolls around again.

Lampasas has held fast and true to its annual festival. Today, it attracts thousands and thousands of tourists. Some visitors are just stopping by, passing through on one of three state highways that barrels through the main drag. Many are coming home. I have no roots there, but I've got a lot of old friends I expect to run into this weekend.

Spring Ho is a great example of what a city can do when all of its forces pull together for a common cause. And, it's a lot of fun.

Adrian Jackson is a freelance writer in Beeville, Texas. She lived in Lampasas for four years.

My spirit soared

I recently saw a performance by Ailey II, part of the Alvin Ailey American Dance Theater. This was not my first time seeing this company, but it had been about 25 years since the last one.

As I watched the performance, my legs shook and my teeth chattered. I put my arms around myself to contain my spirit. The inner me wanted to leap out of my body and join those dancers on stage. My spirit knew that it could move and dance in a way that a physical body - my physical body - was not able to do.

So, I held tight to my spirit, knowing that if I let it go, even for a second, it would not wish to return and be confined by me again.

The dancers splayed, twisted and jutted in ways that defy all laws. Gravity and nature meant nothing. Physics was for the unimaginative. Their bodies shifted effortlessly into poses and positions that seemed unnatural and unbelievable. Their movements seemed driven by souls not to be held back by their corpses. There is not a single word to accurately describe the magnificence of the Ailey II performers. They were beautiful-lovely-handsome-pretty-comely-fair-exciting-sensuous-aesthetic-moving.

I felt privileged to have been a part of the experience. And what an experience it was! I saw the Alvin Ailey American Dance Theater twice prior to the most recent show. The first time was in New Jersey with my mother. The second time was in Harlem on a school trip. I was in awe of the performances back then. Even as a child, I realized the significance of the show.

Alvin Ailey, a native of Rogers (Bell County), Texas, came into dance as a teenager in Los Angeles. He moved to New York where he functioned as a dancer, actor, choreographer and director. He built his dance company from there.

Ailey's style was heavily criticized because it was not classical ballet but a fusion of dance, theater and expressionism. His troupe was heavily influenced by his contemporary dance instructors Lester Horton and Martha Graham. His shows featured, and still feature, athletic dancers with hard bodies that range in color from barely tan to deep chocolate.

His company was afro-centric with performances and music that reflected and celebrated African-American history during a time when nobody else did. Ailey was the first to successfully infuse American jazz, gospels and spirituals into his productions and worked with Duke Ellington and Langston Hughes.

    Ailey is honored and remembered every time his dancers take to the stage. Though he is long dead, his spirit lives on and soars with its companions to songs that reach to my very core. I hope that I'll get to see them perform again in the future.

Kids can learn a lot from the symphony

As a child, I lived within a 20-minute train ride of New York City. I actually grew up in Newark, New Jersey, one of the largest cities on the East Coast.

There are many benefits to living so close to NYC. One is the art and culture. I went to many museum and art gallery exhibits in The City. I got lots of exposure to all kinds of performances – ballets, sporting events and concerts. I saw James Earl Jones in Fences. I went to a Yankees game. I saw an orchestral production of Peter and the Wolf set to a silent, animated cartoon. Being in the tri-state area (New York, New Jersey, Connecticut), I had access to outreach programs that either shuttled inner-city kids to NYC shows or bussed performers out to the surrounding areas and many of my class trips were to Broadway theaters.

Newark, in its own right, is a center for art and culture. When I was a child, we frequented Carnegie Hall. We saw Alvin Ailey's Dance Theater of Harlem and listened to the soulful sounds of Sweet Honey in the Rock. We caught matinees. They were much cheaper than prime-time performances, but the shows were the same. Sometimes, we got to visit with performers who sat down on stage after the show just to talk to us.

There are many opportunities for Bee County kids to take advantage of visiting performers and parents don't even have to travel far. More impressively, these shows are free. Why wouldn't you take your kids to the symphony?

The secret of orchestral, symphonic and operatic music is that we hear it all the time. We hear it in movies like Lord of the Rings and Harry Potter. It is sampled in popular music and we hear it on television shows, commercials and cartoons. Who can forget Elmer Fudd's *Kill the Wabbit*, sung to the tune of Richard Wagner's *Ride of the Valkyries*? The compositions of Oscar-winning composer Hans Zimmer are featured in many animated Disney movies.

There is also a misconception about quiet. Of course, it is polite to be silent and common sense to turn off your cell phone, but toe-tapping doesn't hurt anyone. The symphony is to be enjoyed and appreciated. Kids have to be supervised but not made to behave like adults. And, honestly, these performances are for kids.

Some people think that you have to dress a certain way, but you don't. You just show up and take a seat. When performers come to

Beeville, the cost is much less than the nosebleed seats at the Majestic Theater in San Antonio and a mere fraction of the cost of the good seats. I should know. I just spent $168 dollars for two seats to see *Wicked* in Austin.

I look forward to these visiting performances because it is a great opportunity for me to expand my daughter's knowledge and appreciation of arts and culture. My own mother brought me up the same way and I thank her for making this an integral part of my education and development.

I am looking forward to another theater season in Beeville. Last year's performances were fantastic. There were a lot of kids, but wouldn't it be great if the theater was overrun with schoolchildren?

Where's the #@*%$!!! border?

The worst part about living in Texas is trying to get out if it. The border in any direction is hundreds of miles away.

I recently left Texas for a trip to South Carolina. I packed two coolers, a snack bag, and a book. I'm the sort that only stops to gas up and go. I also stop at visitor centers on the borders. I like to sign the book. But, that is a story for another day.

I left Beeville at one o'clock on a Friday afternoon.

After an hour of driving, I reached Victoria. Not the border.

After two hours of driving, I reached Sugar Land. Not the border.

After three hours of driving, I made it to Houston. Not the border.

After four hours of driving, I hit Beaumont. Not the #@*%$!!! border.

Finally, after *five* hours of driving, I passed mile marker 880 on I-10 and crossed into Louisiana. This is the border. I finally left the great big state of Texas.

If you've never gone out of Texas (and that would be reasonable, since you really can spend your entire life just traveling between Dallas, Austin, Houston, Amarillo, San Antonio and El Paso) you may not realize that this trek is over 300 miles. It is almost one-third of the distance of my journey.

Texas is #@*%$!!! huge. And that's an understatement. There are 509 miles between Beeville and Texarkana. If you drove to Wichita Falls in the north it would be a 439-mile trip. It would take 661 miles to get to El Paso from Beeville and 134 miles to get to Laredo from here. And, those numbers double if you plan to come back.

Well, fast-forward a week. It was time to go home. And as much as I loved the idea of coming home I wasn't that keen on the long drive. But I was wise. I split my trip in half, leaving South Carolina on Friday and spending two days at a friend's house in Louisiana.

My friend lives near I-20, so we didn't cross down through Mississippi to get to I-10 like we usually do. We stayed on I-20.

On early Sunday morning, we left West Monroe, La. for Beeville. I thought we'd find an interstate along the way that would take us from I-20 to I-10. We didn't, but we found Highway 59.

We drove through every eye-blink-you-missed-it town from Marshall to Humble, passing through Nacogdoches, Lufkin, Seven Oaks and Splendora before reaching Houston.

It took us hours and hours and thankfully, the speed limit was not always 55 mph. I wasn't looking forward to the drive, but I didn't have much else to do on a Sunday 400 miles from home. And, I have to admit, the scenery was great.

We drove through the oldest town in Texas. We saw the famous East Texas pines. We saw a giant roadrunner statue at Angelina College in Lufkin and drove past a real locomotive in Diboll. We stopped at a Super Target in The Woodlands. It was a nice drive. I went through places I'll probably never get to again.

In hindsight, there might have been a quicker route through Beaumont, but I'm not that good with maps.

Once I got back to Beeville, I called my sister and told her that I was never driving East again. But, in the back of my mind, I'm already planning a drive west for spring break. There are still big chunks of Texas that I haven't seen yet.

Adrian Jackson is a freelance writer in Beeville, Texas. Her RV dream is to spend a summer driving through Canada and Alaska.

Hoping and praying for rain

One of the earliest things I learned when I got to Texas was to take rain very seriously. There is nothing funny about a rain joke, a rain ditty or anything that will tilt the delicate balance of mojo that controls the weather. It's July and we've had scant few days of precipitation. The recent rain did little more than wet the gauge.

Once when I lived in Central Texas, known for its flash floods and tornados, we experienced about two days of constant and violent rain. It was an answer to many prayers that must certainly have been sent up to God and stored in heaven for years. It was a deluge. We had to sandbag the courtyard square.

It was something to see and people compared it to the Mother's Day Flood of 1957 that destroyed downtown Lampasas. We talked about that rain for weeks and it was the cover story of the local paper for a half dozen subsequent issues. What a blessing it was to hear that in just a couple of days we'd surpassed the previous year's water level.

It was shocking to me to find that though we recovered from that year's drought, we still had 39 years of dry to make up for. 39 years!

It must have taken hearty pioneers to believe that they could scratch out a life in this state. Without weather trackers, there was no way for early Texans to know if it would ever rain and I am sure that many died before ever seeing the skies open up.

Today there are still thousands of Texas ranchers and farmers whose livelihood and fortunes are irrevocably tied to the abundance or lack of rain. So it is no surprise that rain is a frequent topic of discussion. I know many rural Texans who spend time every morning comparing rain gauge results with their friends. One of my friends is the keeper of the official rain gauge for two area newspapers. And if he says there were two inches of rain, it doesn't matter how much more or less you got in your gauge though the topic can be widely discussed.

Having grown up on the East Coast, we prayed for no rain. We sang songs and danced like Indians, hoping we could make it go away. We cursed the sky for ruined picnics, indoor summer days and squishy galoshes. We had no concept of anything less than abundance. We knew nothing of the delicate eco-relationships between the sky and the land that yielded the beef and vegetables on our tables. Rain was a luxury we could afford to wish away.

They recently used fake rain in China. Apparently, they frequently use this technique. It seems like a good idea until you consider the fact that they sprinkle chemical into clouds. Talk about acid rain. Yuck!

Also, if rain increases in one area because of chemical interference, it will decrease in another area because of the forced maturity of clouds. It's like robbing Peter to pay Paul.

Here in Texas, I don't think we are looking to take someone else's rain. We'll get ours honestly. We are watching Hurricane Boris this week. We are hoping that it will not be severe in wind, but plentiful in rain. We are hoping that the rain clouds will cross midline through Mexico and cut a diagonal swath through Texas, drenching us with some much needed precipitation.

We pray for rain in church. When I first heard of a pastor calling for a prayer for rain, I thought he was nuts. I had never heard of such a thing, but I've come to realize the necessity of it. RAIN!!!! is listed on our prayer list.

We are expecting quite a bit of rain in the coming week, but I'll keep praying on behalf of all Texans, for whom the rain is so precious.

Is there a Yellow Rose?

There's a yellow rose of Texas
That I am going to see
No other soldier knows her
No soldier, only me.
She cried so when I left her
It like to broke my heart
And if I ever find her
We never more will part.

What is the story behind the legendary Texas song? Who is the Yellow Rose of Texas?

Emily Morgan or Emily D. West, a young mulatto girl, came to Texas with James Morgan, a seaman and opportunist. It is said that Miss Morgan (or West), who was manager of her master's estate, caught the attention of Mexican General Antonio López de Santa Anna as he marched past Morgan's Point on his way to defeat the Texians.

Emily is said to have unwillingly gone with Santa Anna to his camp where she was forcibly sequestered in his tent. Morgan's presence in the tent distracted Santa Anna enough to give Sam Houston the upper hand. The Texians won the battle, the war and independence from Mexico while Santa Anna was captured with his pants around his ankles. True or not, it makes for a good story.

Some historians believe that Emily didn't exist or, if she did, was a nominal character in the story of Texas, a dwarf in the shadow of David Crockett, Jim Bowie, and Sam Houston. There is plenty of room in Texas lore for legends large and small, so I'm in favor of Emily's status as a legend, but why?

I think she did exist, though her legal status and skin color precludes any legitimate paper trail. Historians say that she was not a slave, but it seems to me that anyone of African descent, regardless of his or her previous status, became a slave upon entering Texas. Whether or not that was explained to Emily who came from New York, I believe that assertions that she was a slave are justifiable ones. What makes her existence probable, in my opinion, is her attachment to names that can be substantiated like Emily de Zavala, wife of a diplomat, and James Morgan. Legends that are solidly attached to events and people are more likely true, at least to some degree.

I believe that she could have been in Santa Anna's tent but I doubt she masterminded a plan to turn the tides of war by keeping the general focused on her body and unfocused on his advancing enemy, as some give her credit for. If he was unfocused because of her, he brought it on himself and I can't fathom any woman who would willingly attach herself to a beanie-wearing, opium-smoking madman though Eva Braun is a close comparison.

I also doubt she was in secret communication with Sam Houston. Though this sort of covert relationship does exist elsewhere in history, I doubt it took place at San Jacinto. If it had, it would have been brilliant, but from a practical standpoint it doesn't seem plausible.

So who is Emily West and what makes her a legend? Was she created to give African-Americans a stake in the sesquicentennial celebration of 1986 as some cynical historians assert. We will probably never know the truth about Emily.

The popular song attributed to her was claimed to have been written and later recorded by a dozen men across the South. I doubt anyone knows where it originated from. It seems a stretch that it was written about her but possible that some soldier who was familiar with the song discovered that this pretty mulatto girl fit the bill and the association stuck.

I say soldier because it is unlikely to me that a black man wrote the song. I don't think that blacks referred to themselves as 'darkies' in the presence of each other the way that today's rappers refer to themselves and each other as 'niggaz.' It is more realistic, in my opinion, that a white man wrote the song (writing being exclusive to whites at the time), maybe about a mulatto to whom he held a dubious attraction for (not an unusual scenario) and used the word 'darkie' to dissipate suspicion of the song's true source.

With more questions about Emily than answers, I still think she is a Texas legend. Her story has mystery, drama and a revolution – the makings of a great story. Though little is known about her, the song conjures up those like her who encompass the spirit of Texas.

Looking forward to traveling the Coastal Bend

When I first visited Corpus Christi in 2001, one of my most eagerly-awaited adventures was horseback riding at Mustang Riding Stables. I rode down the beach on a ginormous animal that didn't mind one bit that I was a novice. My daughter was only three and had to ride with a guide but she had a great time. She has always loved horses.

The ride cost a bit more than I'd planned to spend, but I am glad that I did it. It was a once-in-a-lifetime opportunity. Earlier this year, just months after the death of stables owner Roy Graham, his family decided to close the business and sell off the horses and equipment. Mustang Riding Stables was a landmark for tourists and after 20 years, it is gone. I hope that a similar business will crop up soon in the same area. I'm sure it would also be successful.

Even without the riding stables, there are still plenty of shoreline activities to do in the Coastal Bend. There are public beaches and parks. There are fishing trips and ferry rides. There are many ports and islands to explore. We've been to Port Aransas and Mustang Island, but never to Goose Island or Ingleside.

One of the things that attracted me to this region of Texas was its beautiful beaches. Swimming is great, but watching the aquatic life and collecting shells and sea glass is just as enjoyable. The weather, even at its coldest, is pretty mild. Temperatures have gone up recently making swimming and camping likely activities in the coming weeks.

I don't spend nearly as much time on the shore as I had envisioned I would when I moved to Beeville. Part of the reason for that is life. It is difficult to find time for recreation when you have to work and fulfill obligations like soccer games, performances and school functions that rapidly fill up a calendar. I make a commitment every spring to take in more of the Coastal Bend, but there is still much for me to see and do. There are a lot of day trip opportunities. We try to visit as many state parks as we can and South Texas has its fair share of those.

One thing that I didn't understand when I got here was why you can't get to South Padre Island from North Padre Island. It boggles me. The distance between the two islands is not that great. You'd think there would be a bridge or a ferry or something. And, why can't you take South Padre Island Drive to South Padre Island? Didn't the city planners consider that when they named the road?

I was on South Padre Island a few years ago and figured I'd just drive north to get back to Corpus Christi. I thought that if there was no bridge connecting North and South islands, there would be some kind of connection to an inland road that connected to a northerly road. But, as you know, there isn't one. The only connection is to Highway 77 and wherever you are on South Padre Island, you have to work your way back to the southernmost tip to get to Port Isabel on the mainland.

Remembering Lady Bird

I got the opportunity to go to Johnson City and Austin last week. It was my privilege to sign the condolence book to honor the memory of Lady Bird Johnson.

I was traveling through the Hill Country on Highway 281, so stopping at the national park office was on the way.

I wanted to pay my respects to the woman who greatly impacted our country in civil rights and environmentalism. I went to Head Start in 1975, so I had to honor her for that as well. I also wanted to represent my family and signed the names of my sisters' families, my family and my in-laws in the books that are records of a historical event.

After I left the park office, which, by the way, is a mini-museum and bookstore, I met up with my friend in Lampasas. She said her family was going to the LBJ Library where Johnson laid in repose. My friend invited me to go with them.

My friend and her husband are University of Texas at Austin grads. He was in college when President Lyndon Johnson died in 1972. He was among those who filed past the president's coffin when his body lay in state at the newly-opened library, so the opportunity to pay respects to the president's wife held special significance to him.

My friend's daughter and her roommate are also UT grads and true Austinites. They talked about Town Lake, the wildflower center and the great impact that the Lady had on their home city. My friend's son, a San Angelo State University student, also came along. He'd never been to the LBJ Library.

I'm glad we decided to go to Austin late at night and stand in line. I'm glad that we shared that particular moment together.

Lady Bird Johnson will be remembered as gracious, beautiful, refined and genteel. She will be forever compared to the delicate, but hardy wildflowers she so desperately loved. It is a visually dignified, fitting comparison, but it does not encompass all images of her.

Lady Bird Johnson was booed, hissed, yelled at, spit upon and hit during her campaigns in the South against laws that segregated races and condemned blacks to a lifetime of second-class citizenry. She worked tirelessly for her husband during all phases of his political career, despite criticism and ostracism. She dragged a gaggle of reporters around the country to confront poverty, ignorance and intolerance at its source. She stood up and spoke out against injustice where it lived.

She was highly intelligent. She was educated at a time when it was rare for women to leave home to earn a degree. She was a businesswoman and, when her husband went off to war, she ran his congressional office.

My friends and I had different reasons to honor Johnson as we stood in line on that night in Austin. She was a role model for all women. She was a model of First Ladies. She was an environmentalist and activist. And, through it all, she was a lady.

May she rest in peace.

Becoming a Texan (a lifetime to go....)

If you've ever met me, you know I'm not from around here. As a matter of fact, I just got here about a decade ago. I'm from New Jersey. It's northeast of here.

I've observed the uniqueness of you Texans who take pride in reciting your pledge. I don't know if there is a pledge in New Jersey. I can honestly say I never recited one.

When I attended college here (Central Texas College, Texas Tech University) I found that the story of the Civil War history is very different than what I learned up North. As it turns out, the Southern states weren't entirely to blame. Go figure!

I expected to see cowboys in Texas and I do. But, I didn't expect to see an 85-year-old rancher, covered in caliche, come to town to pay cash for a brand-new pickup. And I can proudly say that not only do I know what caliche is, I am also occasionally knee-deep in it. I expected to hear people say 'Howdy' in Texas and they do. But, I didn't expect the dean of fine arts at Central Texas College to say, 'Ya'll settle down. Class is fixin' to start.' I expected to wear jeans to work in Texas and I do. But I didn't expect to see denims over road-weary, full quill ostrich boots that are custom made to fit your feet. I expected to see horses in Texas and I do. But I didn't expect to see them hitched to handmade Amish buggies.

In my short time here, I've learned that brisket is better with pickles on top, you take your clothes to a washateria, and all roads lead to Gatesville. I've learned that hunters in Central Texas hunt in the south and hunters in South Texas hunt in the Hill Country. I've learned that the stars at night shine big and bright and you don't mess with Texas. I've learned that there are two breed of Texans: Aggies and Longhorns. You are either one or the other and you make your choice as a child and stick with it. A Texan who is both an Aggie and a Longhorn is a rare breed indeed but I've met a couple of them.

I've learned that if Texas were a country its states would include North Texas, South Texas, West Texas, East Texas, The Hill Country, The Valley, The Gulf Coast and Austin.

I've learned that Pedernales is not pronounced the way it looks and the closer you get to the Mexican border the harder you have to trill your 'R's.

I'm probably going to stick out like a sore thumb for another decade or so but I'm getting to know Texas better every day.

Lessons learned while lost in the woods

My ancestors have evolved from cave dwellers to college-educated, city folk who have abandoned hunting and gathering in favor of shopping at super centers. Why, then, would I willingly set up a camp and sleep in a woodland clearing for two days? Hmm? I don't know but somehow I am changed by the experience.

My daughter and I recently visited Lost Maples State Natural Area in Vanderpool, Texas. We backpacked with a group of Girl Scouts and explored the highest and lowest points of the mountainous park. Our group wasn't alone but we had to rely on our wits and supplies for survival. Of course, at any moment, we could have just hiked a few miles down to our vehicles for stuff but let's call it primitive camping anyway.

Lost Maples, old Apache and Comanche lands, is known for its various and colorful foliage, a rarity in Texas. Obviously, the best time to visit is fall but I think our trip was no less spectacular in other ways.

We spent weeks preparing for it. There is a lot of pressure in knowing that you can't run to the store when you need something. Everything we needed had to be contained in two backpacks and one had to be fairly light, since my daughter isn't physically able to lug her fair share. The rule was if you couldn't carry it on your back, you couldn't bring it. Space was a premium and tough choices had to be made.

One of our best decisions was to take a single burner, folding stove, instead of a propane cooker. We cooked surprisingly well on our little stove. We heated U.S. Army Meals-Ready-to-Eat (MREs) one night. We made bacon, eggs and pancakes for breakfast the next morning. We created what has since become our staple camp dinner of chopped carrots, celery, chicken from a pouch and Ramen noodles.

We packed water and frozen juices. The boxes make excellent ice packs. We got our cook and clean water out of the creek. The water was clear and cool and it was fun to have to stand in the creek with tin cups and toothbrushes. There were fish, snakes and leeches in that creek, but it was an invaluable resource.

I wanted to bring my usual two-room tent but found that it was ridiculously large and heavy. There was no way I could fit that big tent into my rucksack. I had to buy a small tent specifically for primitive camping. The tiny tent we slept in involved a lot of crawling around and both my head and feet touched the walls. I had to sleep with a scarf and a hood because I picked up precipitation from the walls of the tent. I hate pup tents and felt that ours was a huge sacrifice for me.

We didn't sacrifice on bathrooms, though. We camped a few yards from an outhouse. It was a two-story model with compost. No more need be said about that.

We took quite a few rocky roads through the park. A 30-minute ascent over a fall of rocks was challenging. Terrain warnings were everywhere, but we were unhindered by them. We are scouts. I relearned the old lessons about adversity and reward. The view from the top was out of this world. Going downhill was as difficult as going up, but we had lunch by a beautiful fishing pond.

In a temporary state where cell phones, play dates and televisions don't exist, my daughter and I had to learn to be a team. We worked side-by-side and had a good time. We laughed, hugged, talked and stumbled more than we've ever done before. We scrubbed dishes in the creek and played cards under the light of a bug-infested lantern. We checked each other for tics and held hands as we clambered over river rock crossings. We learned something about ourselves and each other and formed a new, unique bond.

I drove her on when the trail got long and she waited for me when the road got rough. We learned that even though our camping trip was only sort of primitive, two days in the woods is not such a bad way to spend a weekend together.

Adrian Jackson is a freelance writer in Beeville, Texas. She has rediscovered her love of camping.

Those weirdo livestock kids

When I was a kid we took annual field trips to the New Jersey State Fair. Every summer, we'd have a great time eating cotton candy, buying handmade toys and riding the Ferris wheel. Kids came from across the state to have a good time at the fair. They still do.

Back then, there were a lot of kids at the fair dressed in coveralls. They were showing their animals – horses, sheep, goats, rabbits, chickens, you name it. Those kids seemed to like to wear ribbons and boots and those animals sure smelled like poo. We thought they were all weird.

We were a busload of city kids and if you think we ever got within 20 feet of those kids and their barnyard animals, you are sadly mistaken, pal. We looked at those farm kids like they'd just been dropped off the mother ship.

Well some 20 years later, as a parent of one of those weirdo livestock kids, I've learned quite a bit about a culture that was once so alien to me.

My first livestock show was about four years ago in Lampasas. I immediately noticed the dress code. I've never seen little boys as spit-shined as they are at a stock show. And girls, with their ponytails, are as pretty and fresh-faced as they will ever be. With nary a hair out of place, they all come into the show barn walking ten feet tall.

There is an odd game played in the arena. It's called 'manage your animal, smile and make eye contact with the judge at all cost.' It's peculiar to watch. It's like an awkward dance. It amazes me that there never seems to be any pile-ups.

I'm not an old hand in the show barn, but I can navigate my way through it. I've recently learned that nanny goats have horns too. I know that pigs are smarter than we give them credit for. I know that you're allowed to show a dead chicken.

Having lived in rural Texas for years, I've gotten to know many of the kids involved in 4-H and FFA. They are a great bunch. They work hard getting ready for the stock show. They work for months. Those animals are a huge responsibility. If I ever mistakenly thought the show started when they walked into the arena, I now know better.

I have renewed respect for those kids who work hard for the privilege of showing at the state fair. I understand now that it's not weird, just different. I still can't tell a chestnut from a quarter horse, but maybe there's hope yet for this city kid.

Goodbye, Little Red

The goat is gone. I have to admit I'd grown fond of her. She was a pretty little thing.

Little Red was given to us by the Sachtlebens for my daughter's 4-H project. It was a generous gamble on their part. I had no idea at the time that goats were so expensive and giving us one, even on loaner, was an incredible gift from strangers.

We all knew Little Red wouldn't be a winner, but she was mild-tempered and small. We all believed my daughter could handle her. It was a perfect match for a first show.

With the help of the Taylor family, we brought the goat home. We built a shelter and padded it with hay. We were a little concerned that Little Red would be lonely, but the goats next door would frequently visit and stay longer if we offered them food.

Little Red seemed to like the new digs. She especially liked the tree in her pen. She would lean on my shoulders to reach the leaves.

My daughter bonded with the goat over time. She had to feed her, spend time with her and walk her every day, so there was ample opportunity to get connected. After the newness of it wore off, taking care of Little Red was more like a chore, but my daughter still had fun with it. Me? I could think of better ways to spend my time than raking up goat droppings, but I'm a 4-H parent now.

We called our friend Eric 'the goat master' because he took on the role of supervisor. He took care of my daughter and Little Red as if they were his own. He put in a lot of hours getting the new pair ready for the show and managing his own group of animals.

Over many months, my daughter learned how to walk, stand and manage Little Red. She handled her pretty well. Eric shared some trade secrets with her that no one told him when he was her age. She was ready for the stock show.

They were just adorable in the show ring. Apparently, the show judge wasn't looking for adorable. They didn't even place. Not that any of us cared. For us, the experience was a great success. We all congratulated my daughter on her success.

It was time for Little Red to get on with the next phase of her life. She returned to her owners, missing the fate of many of the other goats in the show.

My daughter didn't cry but became very pensive when she knew it was time to part ways with the goat. She wondered if Little Red was big enough to be a mom. I assured her that the goat would make a great mother. And a pretty one.

I wish Little Red a long and productive life. I thank her for being a part of my daughter's life and for not misbehaving at the stock show.

I thank the Sachtlebens and the Taylors, especially Eric. I thank 4-H and the extension office for making opportunities like this one available for Bee County youth.

Here's how the visit went

My sister's brief stay in the Lone Star State was fantastic! Good food, good fun, a little history and a lot of laughs made up her first trip to Texas.

I picked up my sister and her friend at the airport in Corpus Christi on Thursday evening. They were pretty wiped out so we just gathered around the dining room table. We caught up on high school stuff like bad prom dates and good grades. We went through old yearbooks and exchanged pictures of our children. We didn't stay up very late.

We got up early on Friday and headed to San Antonio. We didn't walk far from the parking garage to reach the Riverwalk. We followed a gaggle of schoolchildren along the river, stopping at street vendors and waving to the boat people. I bought two necklaces with painted Scrabble tiles. My sister bought a postcard from the San Antonio Visitors Center for a little boy in her daughter's class who is working on a project about the state of Texas.

Next, we went to the Alamo. No self-respecting tourist leaves the state without the required visit to the Alamo. We walked around, listened to a lecture and walked around some more. We stayed for a couple of hours and I saw exhibits that I hadn't seen before. I'm not sure if they were new or if I'd just overlooked them in the past.

We took public transportation to El Mercado. The city of San Antonio makes it easy to travel by making trolley buses available to tourists at ridiculously low prices. The four of us rode there and back on a $5 bill. We walked around the market square and had lunch at Mi Tierra before heading home to meet up with my oldest sister, driving down from Killeen, with her kids. My South Carolina sister hadn't seen two of her nephews since they were preschoolers. They are now 18 and 19, both graduating from high school in a few days. It was great that they were able to come down for a visit.

On Saturday, we all set out to have a big family barbecue. A friend gave us a grill for brisket and corn-on-the-cob. My oldest sister made potato salad. I made chicken fajitas and Spanish rice. I bought Charro beans from a local taqueria. I made guacamole, but no one ate it. Apparently my entire family hates avocados. My visiting sister kept fresh margaritas coming all night long with her new-found friend Pepe Lopez (hecho en Mexico).

Surprisingly, Beeville weather didn't hold out and our outdoor party with the hanging candle holders, a *chiminea* with mesquite firewood and fiesta-like atmosphere was a big bust. Instead we darted in and out of the rain to pull meat and veggies off the grill and ate indoors, buffet-style with paper plates.

We got out of the house early on Sunday morning to drive to Galveston. Along the way, we marveled at the miracle that is Sugar Land and ate greasy fried food at a rest stop that served Boudain balls, a Louisiana specialty.

As we were crossed onto the island, we saw a graveyard for wrecked ships and noted that a lot of Galveston residents were living in trailers in front of their homes. There is still much to clean up and repair, but the industrial area and the loading dock for cruises seemed to be back in full swing, as were the tourist-centered businesses. My sister and her best friend boarded their ship and we drove off. It was great fun for me because I've never been that close to a cruise ship before. Before heading back home, we detoured downtown to see the old Victorian homes and then followed the shoreline back to the highway.

When I pick her up from Galveston this weekend, I'll try to squeeze in a short trip to Corpus Christi to show her the Nina, moored at the marina, visit the Selena memorial, and visit the Water Street Market. That's about all we'll have time to do before my sister's 5:30 a.m. flight takes off on Monday morning.

My sister had a great time in Texas. I hope that means she'll come back for another visit.

Adrian Jackson is a freelance writer in Beeville, Texas. Her home was filled to the brim with three sisters, one childhood friend, three teenage boys, an 11-year-old girl, a dog and a cat.

Time for our last hurrah

It's the time of year when my family plans one last trip before we all settle into our fall routines. With work, school, soccer and daylight savings time, it will get increasingly harder to find time to do things before fall ends and the holidays roll around. So, we go on one trip that we call our 'last hurrah'.

I'd like to go to South Padre Island. I've only been once and I was on a business trip so I ate a nice seafood meal but didn't have time for much else. I'd like to take my daughter to see Port Isabel and maybe take a side trip to Brownsville.

I'll consider going back to Galveston. We visited the beach during a weekend trip to Houston. The beaches there are a beautiful sienna color. The sand is very unlike what we have in Corpus Christi. When we took that trip we were able to take the ferry over to the San Jacinto monument. It was a well-spent weekend.

We could daytrip to San Antonio. We used to have memberships to the Witte Museum and SeaWorld but we are both a little burned out of that city. We've never been to La Villita or the Majestic Theater but we've pretty much been everywhere else.

We used to take an annual capitol city tour that included the Capitol building, Bob Bullock State History Museum, Texas Natural Science Museum and the Austin Children's Museum. We would walk down to the water to feed the birds and watch canoes and though my daughter wanted to stay for the bats, I could never get up enough courage to do so.

My daughter's favorite zoo is in Forth Worth. We used to drive up there when we lived in Lampasas. We'd take the scenic route and it never took more than four hours. It would take about nine hours to get there from Beeville, so that's out.

Since my daughter enjoyed camping so much earlier this year and the cost of gas inhibits our ability to travel far, our back-to-school trip may only be as far as Goliad State Park. We'll have to see.

Whenever we need ideas for trips we look at "Insider's Guide: Fun with the Family Texas Edition." This book is a great guide to trips large and small. It's separated by region, so that we can cluster activities within a single area. Over the years we've also used it as a diary. We use stars to rank our favorite places. Sometimes we write in comments. My daughter wrote 'Awesome!' in scrawly second-grade letters next to the Science Place in Dallas.

Of the top ten largest cities in Texas, we've checked off Houston, Dallas, San Antonio, Austin, Fort Worth, Corpus Christi and Plano. We've just got El Paso, Arlington and Garland left on that list. Of the seven geographical regions, we've only been to four. Though we've driven through The Panhandle and The Piney Woods, we did little more than stop for food and gas. We've never been to West Texas. It might be fun to take a trip out there. I'd love to go to the Davis Mountains and the McDonald Observatory.

Whatever we decide to do, I'll tell you how it went.

Adrian Jackson is a freelance writer in Beeville, Texas. Her first trip to Texas was in 1995. She's logged thousands and thousands of miles on Texas highways since then.

A new kind of flower grows in West Texas

Driving north on Highway 84, I came upon an interesting farm. Imbedded in fields of cotton are more than 600 wind turbines moving at the same speed, in the same direction. These modern day windmills went on for miles and miles and miles.

They were situated in neat rows like a well-planted garden. They looked like mammoth flowers or monochromatic spinwheels. They whirled synchronized under the direction of the wind. They moved in languorous, three-pronged circles.

I wondered if the wind turbines made great swooshing noises. I was driving 70 miles per hour and could hear nothing. I wondered if you could feel the draw of the air current or get tugged into the towers' arms if you stood too close.

The Roscoe Wind Farm stretches over several counties. The energy generated by wind turbines across the U.S. provide enough power last year to supply 2 million families, according to the American Wind Energy Association.

The wind turbines appeared out of nowhere in West Texas and continue on for a long time. I've seen wind turbine farms in Germany, where they decorate the landscape up near Cologne, so the sight of them wasn't what held my fascination. It was the fact that we were so close and they seemed to go on forever. At a poignant moment in the drive, I spotted a single, old-time windmill. It stood like a pathetic dwarf in a lonely field surrounded by modern technology. It was *altmodisch* in the pristine wave of white wind turbines.

On the return trip south, I noticed that the landscape was dotted with blinking red lights. They were everywhere, blinking simultaneously. They covered the landscape as far as I could see. It took a while to realize that the dots were wind turbines.

I got an otherworldly feeling driving past them. It was like West Texas was being invaded by an alien spacecraft hovering just above the ground. I felt like Roy Neary in the movie "Close Encounters of the Third Kind." There was a sinister pall over the landscape – the absolute opposite effect that the wind turbines had on me earlier. I was creeped out and wanted to get out of the area as fast as possible.

Adrian Jackson is a freelance writer in Beeville, Texas. She is a graduate of Texas Tech University.

TRAVEL

Oh! The places you'll go

You haven't really traveled until you've had to use the restroom in a foreign country. Forget everything you read in travel books. Using the toilet is the cultural experience. First of all, toilet paper in public restrooms outside of the U.S. takes some getting used to. Rolls are usually brown, rough and made of recycled (hopefully not toilet) paper. Once you accept that the fluffy white stuff is not an option, you are ready to go.

I went to France in the 1990s. There were toilet kiosks on several corners in Paris. To prevent indigent people from making these things one-room apartments, the doors would fly wide open after 15 minutes of occupancy. I never got up the courage to try one out but I'm sure you got bonus points for speed, efficiency and execution.

On Austrian highway, I went to a hole in the ground. Literally. The restroom was nice and clean with proper toilets missing one critical component -- everything under the seat. Let me just say, there was no need to flush and you couldn't if you wanted to.

On a trip to Mexico, I was relieved to find everything under the seat intact but shocked to find no seat. Thankfully, I learned the hover-method years ago. The facilities on buses and airplanes are also challenging. Over the years I've learned two things about bus toilets avoid them at all costs and don't sit anywhere near them. Enough said.

Airplane restrooms require a dance maneuver to enter but are otherwise easy to use. I used to have to coax my daughter into them. She knew what flushing an airplane toilet was like and was traumatized by it. There is also the blue water and the nagging question, 'Where does it go?' Like a bus, if you've been on an airplane for more than five hours avoid the restroom at all costs.

In Germany, in the 1980s, you had to pay a 10-pfenning coin to use the facilities. No matter how urgent your need, you had to jostle a coin out of your pocket and into a door release mechanism. My mother used to line us all up and we'd trade off on the same coin. If you didn't have exact change, well, that's another story. Mercifully, nowadays they just put a coin plate by the door. But you have to contend with some old cleaning lady giving you the evil eye if you give less than 1 Euro.

If you ever get to travel, make using the restroom a part of the experience. You won't regret it. Foreign toilets are an excellent place to go.

I think I see Mickey

If you are looking for me this week, don't bother. I've gone to Disney World.

And let me tell you, for the price I'm paying for this trip, I am having a blast. I'm actually embarrassed to tell you how much this trip is costing me and I haven't even looked over my credit card bill yet.

I told my daughter that this is a once-in-a-lifetime trip for her. I meant that. The next time I go to Disney World, I'll be with my grandchildren and my daughter and her husband will be footing the bill.

My daughter is nine. I decided to take the trip to Disney World now because she's been after me for years about it. I wanted to take her before she got too old to be caught up in the magic and make believe.

This is not my first trip to Disney Word. I haven't been in almost 20 years and a lot has changed since the 1980s. I've changed since then. I was a high school senior. I was 17. I was with friends. I thought a lot of the attractions were goofy and uncool.

Now, I'm 36. I've got a few gray hairs. I'm a mom. I am nostalgic for things that remind me of my childhood. I'm sentimental. I have more fun with my nine-year-old than a busload of people my age.

The last time I went, I completely bypassed Epcot Center. My friends didn't want to go. They thought it was lame. I really wanted to go, but I didn't want to speak out against the general consensus, so I skipped it. I'm not that dumb anymore.

We are spending a day at Epcot. We are seeing as much of the compound as we can squeeze into two days. We are staying in a hotel on the grounds so that we can take advantage of the extra park hours and stick around for the fireworks.

We have cast off reality and immersed ourselves in the fantasy. We are roaming the park wearing mouse ears and Hannah Montana t-shirts. We are snacking on turkey legs and Dilly bars. We are chatting it up with all the princesses and having our pictures taken with cartoon celebs.

It's better than I remember.

Adrian Jackson is a freelance writer in Beeville, Texas. She and her daughter are in Orlando hopped up on sugar and having a ball in the wonderful world of Disney.

I ♥ TEXAS

Texans love to let you know they are Texans. Residents of no other state in the union identify themselves as enthusiastically as Texans. Only New Yorkers are almost as exuberant as Texans but they are mostly celebrating New York City, not state.

I grew up in New Jersey and I've never owned an I ♥ NEW JERSEY t-shirt. Not one. I don't recall a single piece of clothing with the words NEW JERSEY printed on it. Or a cap, mug or bag, for that matter.

On a recent trip to Disney World, I realized how much Texans love to let you know where they are from. I know that Texans in Texas wear a lot of Texas tees, but Texans on the road are also serious about where they are from.

Everybody at Disney World wore t-shirts. I saw the standard pro-team shirts. I saw the run-of-the-mill shirts that represent universities and colleges across the country. I saw a lot of Disney t-shirts. And, I saw a lot of Texas t-shirts.

There were plenty of orange and maroon shirts out there. There was an occasional Texas Tech red shirt (Go Red Raiders!). Edinburg High School band showed up in uniform and later in yellow booster tees. My daughter sported her school shirt (Trojans in the hizzouse! Whoop! Whoop!).

Tourists love to buy shirts from Texas. But Texans also love to buy Texas gear. I know a guy in Beeville who wears a different Longhorn shirt every day. You don't see that in other states. Nobody walks around Racine dressed in Wisconsin t-shirts (I know that because I visited Racine and didn't see a single state-inspired shirt).

At Disney World, I saw Aggie broken-horned shirts and one t-shirt featuring a Longhorn wearing a mortarboard (recent grad, I guess). I saw TEXAS emblazoned across shirts, flags on some and lots of Texas high school gear.

Texas has a unique brand of individualism. It's great because people outside of Texas admire that about Texans. I didn't see a single other state represented by t-shirts. I'm sure there were people there from all over the world, but only Texans clearly stood out. Go Texas!

Adrian Jackson is a freelance writer who lives in Beeville, Texas. Her recent 3,000-mile vacation took her through Texas, Louisiana, Mississippi, Alabama, Florida, Georgia and South Carolina.

Forget Paris

I firmly believe that everyone should leave the country at least once in their lives. Even if you stay on this continent or travel no farther than south of the border, you should get a firsthand look at how others live. Even if you are going to the world's worst tourist trap, go. Get out of the U.S. You'll appreciate your homeland even more.

I've traveled quite a bit since high school. I spent most of my time in Europe but I've been a few other places too. I've done the typical tourist stuff. There is nothing wrong with that, especially if you are unfamiliar with your host country or you don't speak the language. I've done some unique traveling too.

I've traveled enough to be able to compare and contrast. Here are my faves:

Heidelberg, Germany. It has been a college town for hundreds of years. Heidelberg University, chartered in the 1400s, is as much an integral part of the history of the city as the castle that overshadows it. Every August, The Student Prince is performed on the grounds of the castle. The city is host to many cultural events and the home of the Heidelberg Press.

Prague, Czechoslovakia. I normally don't care for major cities but this one stands out for its history and beauty. Its buildings, among them the oldest Jewish synagogue still standing in Europe, collectively fuse classic European with modern Russian architecture. The Charles Bridge is the largest castle in the world. Like most major cities, Prague has a strong cultural center but it is edgier and more *avant garde* than others. It is the middle of a post-Communism democracy so there is a civic freedom vibe palpable throughout.

Temple Bar, Dublin, Ireland. Neither a temple nor a bar, this section of the city is the cultural center. In the daytime, you can find fun shops, taverns and galleries. St. Patrick's Cathedral is nearby. In the evening, it's party central. Pubs and bars stay open and full all hours of the night. Dublin is pretty easy to navigate and of course, they speak English. Ya gotta get a Guinness.

Venice. Time is running out for the city on the sea. It smells bad and is very touristy, but Venezia is a unique and beautiful place. And, there's plenty to shop for.

Garmisch, Germany. Winter or summer, this is the place to go. It is a small Bavarian town. There's skiing, hiking and at 5 o'clock every day the cows come down from the hills and stop downtown traffic.

Garmisch and its neighboring sister, Partenkirchen, was the site of the Winter Olympics of 1936.

Monterrey, Mexico. This interior city is very old-world. There are sculptures everywhere in the city and every bridge is a work of art. There is a great commitment to architectural beauty. There are rows of soccer fields along the highway. There is a national museum, a planetarium, a brewery and a baseball museum. A riverwalk has been recently added. Monterrey is old meets new at its absolute best.

Mallorca, Spain. It's a small island with two distinct regions. One side is predominantly for English speaking tourists. The homes of the rich and famous are there. Frédéric Chopin and his lover Georges Sand spent time on the island in an abandoned monastery in Valdemossa. The other side of the island, where Palma is located, is mostly German-speaking tourists. The food is rich and you can buy terra cotta dishes cheap. The dirt is a beautiful red; olive trees are abound; and there are magnificent caves to explore.

Strasbourg, France. It is an international city and has changed hands many times. It is in the Alsace region, one of the most beautiful regions of Central Europe. It is the capital of the European Parliament. There are beautiful Roman aqueducts visible from a boat down the Ill River. Strasbourg is also known for its wine in a distinctive bottle.

Brussels, Belgium. I love this city and it took me years to visit. This is the ultimate international city where signs are in multiple languages and no one speaks less than two. I gained six pounds in Brussels from eating crème brûlée and drinking fancy coffees for a week. I was fortunate enough to catch the light show at the Grand Place. Belgium is famous for fresh seafood, chocolate, nightlife, museums, history, lace and *Manneken Pis*.

Salzburg, Austria. You can ski the Alps or have coffee at a sidewalk café. There are equal portions of Mozart and Sound of Music and the pastry is perfection. I mean perfection. It is very easy to walk or take the street car around the city and there are plenty of parks and gardens to stop in. There are early Christian cave churches hidden in the hills of Salzburg and traces of the brief American occupation during WWII.

Airport lounge visit yields more than free snacks

A funny thing happened on the way to Texas last Sunday.

It all started earlier this year when I received two free passes to an airport club lounge. I saved the passes to use as an indulgence for when I travelled alone. I decided not to share them with my daughter, my frequent traveling companion.

So, on my way back from Germany after having dropped my daughter off for the summer, I visited the club lounge at Newark Liberty Airport. I sat down with a cup of water and a mug of coffee. I realized that I couldn't see the wall clock, so I moved to another section of the circular lounge. As I sipped my coffee I scanned the lounge – just people watching. I noticed a woman sitting in another section of the lounge. I thought she looked familiar.

There was half of a room and two panes of glass between the woman and me, so I could stalk ... I mean, observe ... her pretty unobtrusively. I stared at her for a long time, mentally convincing myself that she was one of the stars of my favorite radio show – The Satellite Sisters.

I wrote about the show a few months ago. If you are still not listening to the show at www.satellitesisters.com, what is wrong with you? Five real sisters tackling the world one cup of coffee at a time? Believe me, if you read my column you are in the demographic.

Now, I have to tell you that the heart stops for about five seconds between fantasizing that the person you're staring at is a celebrity and actually realizing that she probably is one. The moment that you realize that you've spotted a celebrity that is on your most-likely-to-enjoy-a-drink-with-in-an-airport-lounge list (as opposed to maybe running into Paris Hilton from the most-likely-to-let-her-dog-wet-on-my-shoes list) is both surreal and thrilling.

I was feeling plucky, so I got up, grabbed my carry-on, rounded the corner and approached the woman. 'Um... excuse me... are you Liz Dolan?'

And you know what?! She was! She actually was! She invited me to sit down. What's more? She knew who I was. After I told her my name and said I was a big fan of the show (doesn't everyone say that?), she said, 'Oh, Adrian Jackson, the columnist, right?' At that moment, I was flying higher than I had on the plane from Frankfurt.

Not that my column has ever been published in any newspaper that Liz has ever read. She knows me because I blog regularly on

SisterSpot, the Satellite Sisters' blog site and my call name is 'adrian jackson, columnist.'

So, for about an hour, I had a fantastic conversation with Liz about my flight, my dog, my daughter, my sisters and my plans for the summer. There was a little uncharacteristic prattling on my part but I was excited and afraid that the moment would end too soon. I was cool enough not to gush over the show like a goofy teenager, but I think I demonstrated my level of fandom by recognizing the inside jokes.

Liz was gracious, delightful and fantastic. There was some lively banter, laughing and finishing of each other's sentences. She talked about a new segment of the show and showed me a video clip that hadn't gone live yet. She talked about growing up with four sisters and three brothers. She talked about the presidential election. She told me to have a good trip back.

When I checked the website the next day, I found that she'd blogged about our little encounter. How cool was that?

I didn't use the second free pass. After an experience like that, what could I have hoped to gain with access to another club lounge? Free cheese?

Greetings from the airport

Dressed in pin-striped slacks and high-heeled sandals, I am on my way to Germany today. I always dress up for air travel. My first international trip occurred when I was 17 years old. I flew with two of my sisters. We were dressed in jeans and sneakers but the shoes were new and the clothes freshly pressed. That is how we were taught to travel.

Air travel is a sophisticated mode of transit. It is as glamorous as a cruise or a train. With a ticket in my hand, I become an international traveler. A jet-setter. I am elegant and refined. I speak many languages. My heels click smartly as I make my way through terminals around the world.

Oh, who am I kidding? Sophisticated? Really?!

I arrive at the airport two hours early and still find that there is not enough time to check in my luggage or go through security. I stand in line with no less than 500 other people who all seem to be carrying hand lotion and wearing combat boots. And we are all – every one of us – about to miss our flights.

When I get thirsty, I have to pay $4 for a bottle of water that I could have paid $1 for had I been allowed to bring it in from the outside. Of course, bottled water at McDonald's inside the airport is a little cheaper, but sells out fast and I'd have to wait in line for 45 minutes before gaining that bit of information.

When I get ready to board the plane I have to fight families with strollers and carseats who are no longer able to pre-board and old men who walk with their hands on their hips so that their bent elbows create a parameter around their persons. I have to walk sideways to pass, risking the possibility of flipping over the mountain of baby items some family has compiled in the center of the concourse.

When I get on the plane I find that there is one bag of pretzels per row, so I have to fight for one of maybe ten in a bag. I used to turn my nose up at people who travel with food but now I befriend them. They don't have to gnaw on the floatation device until either the flight attendant tosses a bag of snacks into coach to watch the natives tear each other apart for it or the plane lands.

When I land, regardless of how tired I am, I have to walk five miles to the area where my suitcases have yet to arrive on the carousel. The 300 people I spent the night with are all awake and cranky and now queue up with weapons – luggage carts – that they use to prevent me from getting anywhere near the belt. When my suitcases arrive, one by one, I have to chase them around the room and vault over people's heads to grab them and drag them away before they go back into the dark place from whence they came.

And finally, there is customs. I have to stand in line weighted down, smelly, tired and in a very bad mood. The fact that I am a U.S. citizen has no bearing on the time it will take me to get through customs at home or abroad. I try to act natural so as not to arouse suspicion since this is the only plan I can devise to avoid having suitcases opened and rifled through by customs police.

Air travel ain't what it used to be. If you'll excuse me I think my flight is boarding.

Body search is too personal

When he told me that I could take off my shoes if I wanted to, I should have just taken the stupid shoes off. Instead, I decided to go through the checkpoint wearing black loafers with big metal buckles. Needless to say, the machine went off and I was pulled out of line for a body search.

I realize that airport security personnel have a tough job and they have a very good reason for doing it well. I realize that people hide weapons in all sorts of places and a thorough search is necessary. I realize that anyone could be a terrorist, but come on! If I were a terrorist, would I be carrying a camera bag, a portable DVD player, two carry-on bags, a stuffed animal, a pink blanket, two jackets with matching gloves and scarves, and dragging a 10-year-old behind me? Would I??!

But there I was at Frankfurt International Airport standing on the special mat so that everyone could see that I was – for a short time -- a suspected terrorist.

I assumed the position and was approached by a woman in uniform. She ran her hands across my arms and into my armpits. She wasn't so much patting me down as given me a spa treatment.

She ran her hands slowly down my breasts, my stomach and my sides. Then she knelt down. She patted my legs and then stuck her hand up my pant legs. My ankles appeared to be terror-free, so she ran her hands up my thighs to a place my sister calls 'shenanigans.'

Nope. No weapons there.

Then she ran her hands across my waist and down my pants. That's right, down my pants. *Hey, honey I don't even know your name,* I wanted to say. I wanted to tell her that in some cultures we'd be a considered a couple. But you can't say that standing on the terrorist's mat. You can't be sarcastic or funny or upset or angry.

Apparently, you can be humiliated but you'd better shut up about it. I didn't say a word. I even smiled at her while thinking some very terrorist-inspired thoughts about her.

After getting the okay, I walked away feeling violated. How dare she pull me out of line and search me in that way? Why did I have to be searched? Why didn't the guy in front of me with the neck tattoo get searched? He hadn't taken off his shoes either. What about the long-haired, hippie weirdo? What about the Middle-Eastern guy surrounded by five heavily-covered women? Why didn't any of them get searched?

Was I picked because I was the antithesis of the profile of a terrorist? Was I a (quote-unquote) random selection? Or, was it really just because I didn't take off my shoes?

When I was in my 20s, I was a target for airport security. I looked like the sort of naïve young woman who would take a package from a complete stranger and carry it on board the plane or let someone else pack my suitcase the night before the flight. I was always the one they pulled out of line. Back then, airport security personnel would stick their hands into your bags and rifle through pulling out your underpants and hair curlers for all of the world to see. In hindsight, that wasn't so bad.

It is difficult to support airport security when someone's hands are down your pants. But, we must all do our part to defeat terrorism. The next time I travel I will be a little more wary of airport security personnel and when someone says that taking off my shoes is optional, I'll just take them off.

Adrian Jackson is a freelance writer who lives in Beeville, Texas. She is not a terrorist.

Give me a 'chute; keep your floatie

I used to be afraid of flying. It took me ten years to get over that. It never stopped me from traveling; I was just afraid that every rattle and creak was the herald of my demise. I would even get nervous when I couldn't hear anything on the plane. It gets pretty quiet up there at night.

Air travel seems to fly in the face of God (pardon my pun). How presumptuous are we, who were never equipped to exist above the planet, to have fashioned our own wings. We've built a most unlikely contraption that rivals any bird in its grace and wingspan. We've created a machine that can hurl as many as 800 of us into the skies at our purposeful command. And by we, I mean the Wright brothers and all of the pilots who came behind them. I didn't actually do anything.

I used to pray fervently on planes. I would look for nuns and small children, believing that God granted them immunity from plane crashes and by extension I would be safe too. I used to drink liquor while flying so that I could slip away in an blissful stupor. I'm not as intense as I used to be. They've got better television up there than ever. A good airplane can keep you entertained for hours.

Now, I sit calmly in planes and I even sleep through takeoffs and landings. I am comforted by the knowledge that air travel is safe and pilots don't want to crash any more than passengers do. And if a plane should happen to crash, most on board would likely die quickly.

What perplexes me about air travel are flotation devices. Why do we have them and how are they going to be of any help in a crash? Is it more likely that a plane will go down over water than over land? What if it is a land-locked flight? How are those floaties going to save me in that situation?

Why isn't there a parachute under every seat of the plane? Now there's something I can use. A parachute seems to me to be a helluva lot more useful than those yellow slides that float when they are detached. I've never actually jumped out of an airplane but I'm pretty sure that when pressed I'd take the plunge. It's not like I'll land in a barn behind enemy lines. Even with a few broken bones, my chance of survival is greatly improved. All things being equal, I'll take a parachute over a flotation device any day. Sure, I know the slides have a life-saving purpose, but I think I'll take my chances with a parachute, a whistle and a slight shove.

Watching people to pass the time

I love to watch people in public places. Humans are remarkable creatures in their diversity and complexity. They come in all shapes, sizes and colors. Some are short and some are tall. Some are fat and some are thin. Some have disabilities that are apparent and visible; others are affected on the inside, hidden from view. Some are white; others are black. Still others are brown or yellow or red. Honestly, I never see any green or purple people.

Airports are the best places to watch people. And here I sit, today, watching people go by. Some walk; others run. Some are weighted by kids, computers and carry-ons. Others are free of accoutrements. Some have the nervous look of first time travelers. Others are breezy and sophisticated as if flying is an everyday occurrence.

Their destinations are as diverse as the people themselves. Some are coming while others are going. Some are at home; some are abroad. They are traveling north, south, east, west and all points in between. Some travel alone. Others travel in pairs, sets or big groups.

Airport people are a happy bunch. Not those people at the ticket counter. They are angry. And not those people coming off that plane. They are tired. But in general, people in airports are happy. They are excited about where they are going and most often they are going to happy places like vacation, college and home. Some are going on adventures. Others are starting new jobs, new relationships or new lives. Some are reconnecting with family, old friends and familiar places. They are happy. You can see it in their faces. Even those returning home are still high on memories of happy trips.

I like to make up stories about where people are going and where they've been. When you are a casual observer you have the luxury of knowing nothing and imagining everything. You can create a whole world from a seat in an airport terminal.

The man sitting across from me is dressed in an expensive suit. I think he is an international businessman. He is young, handsome and has the aura of someone who thinks he owns the world. He speaks Italian but I know he is American because of his accent. But maybe his grandmother is from Firenze so his inflections are accurate. I don't know what he's saying but I imagine that he is telling a client to make an offer right away to secure a dream villa in Tirrenia.

The man sitting by the window with a little girl on his back and a baby in his arms is flying home after a vacation with his parents in

Florida. He is the primary caregiver. His wife works for a stockbroker and couldn't get the time off. He's got the legs of a runner, so maybe he used to have a successful career as a personal trainer but he gave it up to raise his kids – a job that he dearly loves.

    The soldier sitting alone at a coffee bar is going home. She was in Afghanistan just three weeks ago and has trouble remaining calm in crowded places. I can tell by the way her eyes dart around that she is tired and uncomfortable. She's closer to home than she's been in two years and she knows there are dozens of family members and friends waiting for her just outside of the gate with signs, flags and yellow ribbons. She's got one more flight to take before ending a journey that took her halfway around the world and back.

A privilege for whom?

Southwest Airlines recently announced that it has discontinued its policy of allowing travelers with small children to pre-board. Are they kidding?! Someone at Southwest Airlines has convinced the powers-that-be that the pre-boarding of parents with little kids is a *privilege*. Let's just go out on a limb and say that *Someone* doesn't have kids and *Powers-that-be* don't either.

For those of us who have kids and will travel, let's look at the truth of the matter. First of all, let me say that I no longer take advantage of pre-boarding.

My daughter is now nine and is expected to behave like a young adult. Besides that, she is a well-seasoned traveler and knows how to move in an expeditious manner. However, she was once a toddler.

When we traveled, we were not limited to a carry-on and a purse. We had to take a car seat, a purse, a diaper bag, a snack bag, a stuffed animal, a blanket, a stroller and a toy bag with us. This was all basic needs. Nothing superfluous on board. We usually traveled alone, so it was me carrying all of this crap plus a baby. And it was a rare occasion when I got help from the airline staff.

Once I got to the gate, I stood as close to the entrance door of the plane as humanly possible. Not that I was trying to get the best seats. I just wanted to get into the belly of the whale before other passengers started shoving me and leaping over my stuff. *You know who you are.*

I wanted to get my belongings situated above the seats, under the seats and in front of the seats so that I could get my daughter strapped in and quieted down before the others came along.

I also wanted to get away from 20-something execs who gave me evil eyes when my daughter spilled dried cereal into leather laptop cases, crawled over Jimmy Choos or screamed at the top of her lungs for no reason at all. These were probably the same young execs who griped to the powers-that-be about privileges.

My seat was never in the front of the plane. It was always in the middle where I had to beg some whiny fat guy to please give up his window seat so that my daughter and I could sit together. This would always wind up with me hitting him in the head with the diaper bag and him stomping off and demanding to be reseated in first class. Talk about privileges!

Even if the flight was uneventful, which it never was, I still had to disembark. This involved the re-packing of bags, the waking of daughter and the dragging of tired self off of the plane to the ugly stares and rude comments of everyone else on the plane, including the not-so-sympathetic flight crew. And I never, ever got off the plane first.

So Southwest Airlines, if you think that not allowing parents with kids to pre-board will level the playing field, then fine. I hope your playing field is strewn with Cheerios and juice boxes. And if you think that not allowing parents with kids to pre-board will speed up the boarding process, then fine. I hope your passengers enjoy obstacle courses. The parent near the boarding gate leaning under the weight of travel gear and a stroller doesn't need your privileges - she needs your compassion.

New Jersey is where the heart is

What do Jerry Lewis, Jon Bon Jovi, John Stewart and I have in common? We are all from New Jersey. No matter how long I live in Texas or anywhere else in the world, I am a Jersey girl at heart. Not to be confused with 'New Joisey.' Everyone outside of the NJ swears we all talk like that, but we do not. We say 'New Jersey,' same as y'all.

We do, however, say dawg (dog), cawa (car) and cawfee (coffee). We say awnt and fawther. My accent has softened over the years, but many pronunciations remain.

The last time I visited, my daughter asked, 'Mommy, why are you talking like that?' When I'm in New Jersey, I sound like a Jersey girl. I slip back into the old tongue.

The Garden State recently inducted 15 New Jerseyans into the new Hall of Fame, located in the state capitol of Trenton. Bruce Springsteen, one of our most popular native sons, was among those honored. Springsteen put Freehold and Asbury Park on the map.

Other honorees were U.S. astronaut Buzz Aldrich; General Robert Wood Johnson II, WWII hero and part of the Johnson & Johnson family; award-winning actress Meryl Streep; and Gulf War General Norman Schwartzkopf.

Clara Barton, a Civil War nurse and founder of New Jersey's first free public school; Albert Einstein, a Princeton University scientist and mathematician; and Thomas Edison, a Menlo Park inventor; were inducted in the Historical category.

Malcolm Forbes, publishing icon, was named in the Enterprise category. Forbes, who grew up in Lawrenceville and later graduated from Princeton, is a former state senator. Frank Sinatra, born in Hoboken, was inducted in Arts & Entertainment. Yogi Berra, whose museum is at Montclair University, was inducted in Sports, along with former U.S. Senator Bill Bradley, who played for the Knicks, and Vince Lombardi, who was once a high school football coach in Englewood.

The General category included Toni Morrison, Nobel Prize and Pulitzer Prize winner, and Harriet Tubman, who lived on Cape May.

While I'll probably never live in New Jersey again, I spent the first 18 years of my life there. My parents and grandparents were born and raised there too. Many still live there.

My mother lives in Carney's Point, Bruce Willis' hometown. My grandmother lives in Newark.

OPINIONS ON EVERYTHING

My cup runneth over

The only thing worse than having things fall into your shirt is having to retrieve them. You may have to check with Miss Manners on this one, but except in an emergency, I think it is very impolite to publicly root around in there on an archaeological expedition. It brings unnecessary attention to you and is a little embarrassing for everyone else.

Your only option is to hold on to whatever is in there until you are in a position to get it out. That's what I do. I can't tell you how many nights I've undressed myself and found chips, fairies and jumper cables tumbling out of my blouse. It is a bit of an annoyance.

Some women purposely use their cleavage as a storage facility. I had an aunt who kept a change purse in there. Whenever she needed cash, she'd fish in there and pull out money. She didn't even have to retrieve the purse. She just popped it open and money appeared. She may have been the inspiration for the automated teller machine.

Some people, like Dolly Parton and Pamela Anderson, have made careers on large breasts. Childbirth ruined any hope I had for a successful career centered around my cleavage and I can't imagine being objectified in that manner, but who am I to criticize others? Parton and Anderson have made billions.

There is certainly a market out there for that sort of thing. Why else would zillions of women subject themselves to surgical enlargements? Even Dolly Parton has admitted to having some ... er, horizontal realignment.

I don't begrudge women for having cosmetic surgery. If you have the means to make improvements, why not make them? If you are unhappy with something and can change, go for it.

Breast enlargements are fairly common nowadays. They aren't regarded as something bad, wrong or secret. It is interesting to see many women who are not naturally endowed go for the greater cup sizes. I can't imagine willingly taking on more than I can carry.

What must it have been like before cosmetic surgery? Underclothes prior to the 1970s seem to have been more battlements than garments. Their primary function seems to have been to protect the wearer from marauders. High and dry seemed to have been held in high regard. Whatever the purpose, undergarments looked neither comfortable nor flattering.

Flattening, however, is a different subject. Girdles and corsets were the cosmetic surgery of generations past. A stomacher was the Edwardian Mommy-lift. Spandex was the nip-and-tuck of the 1980s. What Lycra in the 1960s, put together let no man put asunder without the consent and assistance of a full-figured woman.

School kids face serious dangers

Our kids aren't safe at school anymore.

School is the one of the very few places I leave my child. I supervise her activities. I sit on the sidelines during her practices. I attend her friends' birthday parties. When I can't be with her I leave her in the care of someone I trust.

But I leave her at school. I drop her off and drive away. And I put my trust in people who are qualified by the state to look after her. I have to believe that she is safe from harm -- physically, mentally and emotionally. If I didn't believe that, I would never go to work.

When I was in grade school, the biggest threat I ever faced was a 12-year-old third grader who wanted to rearrange my face. I was terrified, but looking back, it was nothing.

But today's schoolchildren are confronted by teachers who want to engage them in sexual relationships. They are faced with vigilantes who find death the only fitting retribution for inconsequential slights. They are photographed by adults with high speed digital cameras and zoom lenses that invisibly reach across playgrounds.

Girls have to deal with boys who drag them into restrooms and take from them what no one should be forced to give. Boys have to put up with girls who subjugate their bodies in a manner that grown women find shocking and tasteless.

Threats from bullies are no longer idle and pose a real concern for parents. Cliques are as treacherous and destructive as gangs. Fights are frequently sadistic and debilitating. Weapons in school aren't uncommon.

There are drug dealers in our children's classrooms. There are thieves and convicts. There are bomb threats. There are schoolchildren with no regard for human life.

I've lulled myself into a sense of security because I live in a small town. I watch school violence on the news and think that won't happen here. That only happens in big cities. That only happens in high schools. That only happens to other people's kids.

The truth is that it can happen. It can happen here. I don't know what to do with that knowledge. It terrifies me.

My only recourse is prayer. Honestly, what else can I do but ask God to keep my little one safe and thank Him for delivering her back to me at the end of the day? School is supposed to be a nurturing and secure environment, but school is more likened to the lion's den.

You'll get blind trust from me

[Note to reader: If you are an auto mechanic, doctor or pharmacist please do not read this.]

I spoke to an auto mechanic the other day. He said my car needs a clock spring. He said he wasn't positive it would fix my problem but he was pretty sure that it would. I nodded. I asked him about four questions. Since I spoke very slowly like I had given this situation a lot of thought, he may not have realized that I'd just repeated what he'd told me, but in the form of questions.

There are few places in this world where I feel out of my element or insecure or stupid, but when I'm at the car repair shop I feel all three. This is one of those situations where the person you're speaking to knows so much more than you that you are forced to nod frequently and agree with everything he says. There is a lot of trust involved in this relationship.

The doctor's office is another one of those places for me. *What? There's one in a gazillion chance that this could cause cancer? It needs to be removed? Today? Um, yeah, okay.* 'Cause the truth of it is who the heck am I to argue with a doctor? He gets blind trust from me. I never have questions. I don't even want a second opinion.

Pharmacists get blind trust from me too. If she is wearing a white coat, I'm secure in the knowledge that she is qualified to do her job. I think she uses big fancy words just to impress me. It works. I wouldn't even know where to begin to question a pharmacist. My most frequent question goes: *Is there a generic brand of this stuff?*

Some professionals like politicians and teachers get nothing but questions. They are always being second-guessed by smart alecks, know-it-alls and those who think they can do a better job. These guys can't catch a break.

People don't ask me a lot of questions in my line of work. I guess they are pretty secure in their assumption that I know what I'm doing. Some genuinely have no idea of what I do, so I'm insulated in that regard. I wouldn't want to be a politician or a teacher. Always with the questions. Oy!

How much is too much?

Does an All-You-Can-Eat sign give you permission to eat all you can?

I listened to a radio news story about a $40 All-You-Can-Eat special at a baseball stadium. The catch? You could only get four hotdogs at a time and it was over by the seventh inning.

The interviewer spoke to some guy who was well over 300 pounds. He'd picked up four dogs and 2 plates of nachos, plus bags of peanuts and popcorn. He said he could eat as many as eight hotdogs and hoped he wouldn't get a stomachache. He wanted to get more than his money's worth.

Another interviewee packed down four hotdogs. She was petite, but thought it was funny to stuff down three more before the end of the day.

One pair of buddies was upset because a snack stand ran out of hotdogs. Instead of giving up, they sought another snack stand. One said he could eat 10 hotdogs. And, he didn't mind standing in line.

How much is too much?

If you've ever been to a buffet (and who hasn't) you'll see some hefty plates and multiple trips. Some of us are willing to eat ourselves sick just because we can get away with it. It's disgusting.

If I walked into a bank and the teller gave me a bag and said I could keep all I could carry, I'd near kill myself stuffing that bag with cash. But when it comes to my stomach, my body and my health, I tend to pull back a little.

I admit that I usually eat more at an All-You-Can-Eat buffet than I would at a regular meal. I also eat more than I need to stay healthy. I am overweight. But, I don't sidle up to a buffet like it's a stand-off. *It's me or you, General Tsao*. I don't serve a full plate of appetizers, a heaping plate of food and a plate of four or five desserts.

I know when to say enough is enough. I don't leave a stack of dirty plates on the table. I don't have to digest for an hour before I can stand.

There is such a thing as too much. We need to recognize limits. We need to stop and think about what we are doing to our bodies. What are the physical consequences of eating 10 hot dogs in one meal? Yuck!

Adrian Jackson is a freelance writer in Beeville, Texas. Her struggle with weight is a daily battle.

The death of a servicemember

Somewhere in America a soldier recently returned home in a box.

As he was laid to rest a group of people from across the country gathered. Not to mourn his death but to hold up signs proclaiming, "God Hates Fags!"

It doesn't matter what your views on homosexuality are in this situation, how did we as a society allow this to happen?

The death of a soldier is always a tragedy. No soldier deserves to die yet they all line themselves up shoulder to shoulder knowing that they won't all get to return home when the fighting is over.

When any soldier dies we mourn. We understand that the life of a man or woman willing to sacrifice his life, liberty and pursuit of happiness in the selfless act of serving his country is all the more precious.

We honor our servicemembers. We honor them with acts of kindness, prayer, care packages, respect. We honor them with signs of solidarity like yellow ribbons, U.S. flags and car stickers. We celebrate Veterans' Day and Memorial Day. We list the names of those who've died in the service to our country on monuments in courthouses, parks, cemeteries and schools.

This is what we do. But, who are the people who travel to the funerals of servicemembers to protest homosexuality?

Sure, we have the right to protest. We have the right to speak freely even when others don't agree or even want to hear what we have to say. But at what point does our right to protest outweigh dignity, honor and respect for someone who lost his life in the service of his country? At what point do the words of protestors become more important that those of eulogizers?

With the right to free speech comes conditions. The conditions aren't defined by the Constitution. Our forefathers didn't have the foresight to fathom that we'd use our constitutional rights to protest at a funeral. Society defines the conditions.

We collectively decide what can be said by determining what we will listen to. We decide through enactment of laws who will be protected from rampant free expression. We set limits of what is acceptable. There are lines that we've decided will not to be crossed.

I think decency should prevent protestors from disturbing a funeral. I think morality should keep people from upsetting the mourning process. I think our servicemembers deserve our gratefulness and respect long after their lives have ended. Not everyone feels this way apparently.

Does God hate fags? I don't know. I don't need an answer to that question. Does God hate people who dishonor those who've lost their lives in service to their country?

Ear worms are taking over the world

I've got ear worms for which there is no cure. I get ear worms that last for hours, days and weeks without end.

I like to move it, move it.

Ear worms are those annoying snippets of songs you hate that get trapped in your head. I am inundated with mind-numbing lyrics to pointless songs and hypnotizing jingles that ricochet around my brain.

Physically fit, physically fit, physically, physically, physically fit.

I've found that I seldom know more than two lines of whatever song is making its way through the grooves of my arbor vitae like poisonous vines straggling the life out of clear thought. Either those two lines loop indefinitely or I make up words to move the tune along. No matter what I do, the song remains.

Unless, of course, it is replaced by a more annoying song. I've heard that an effective way to get rid of an ear worm is to replace it by something worse like the theme to Gilligan's Island. What's a more powerful ear worm than that?

Just sit right back and you'll here a tale.

I don't remember having this problem 20 years ago. I wonder if music has gotten worse or is there just less going on up in my noodle? I suspect music, in all media, is more pointless than it ever. I think songs are more commercial and less soulful than they used to be and the more likely a listener is to remember the jingle or catch, the more commercially successful a song is.

It's bananas. B-A-N-A-N-A-S.

I feel like I'm overwhelmed by it. The onslaught of stupid music is out of my control. I think there are studies going on in secret research and development labs. They are coming up with ways to numb our brains and turn us into zombies. Pinky and The Brain are going to take over the world while we are all humming *I wish I were an Oscar Meyer Weiner*. It could happen. How would you know?

My bologna has a first name.

Where's my defense? It's not like turning off the television or radio will help. Have you been shopping lately? They play music. They preview music videos and show commercials. They loop Paula Deen cleaning pots with lemons. There is no place to hide.

'Cause Oscar Meyer has a way with B-O-L-O-G-N-A.

Run for your lives!

It's summer. How're your feet?

It's almost summer. That can only mean one thing – feet. People across the nation are shucking off socks and closed-toed clunkers in favor of flip-flops, mandals, and Birkenstocks.

The common factor in footwear is feet and whether you want to or not, you're going to get an eyeful.

I happen to be uncomfortable with feet. I am learning to love my own but will never love another's. But since they are out there, here's what I do not want to see:

- **White feet.** Unless you are an albino, there is no excuse for white feet. If you cream your feet before you go to bed or before you put on your shoes in the morning, you will save the rest of us the misfortune of seeing such an aberration.
- **Crusty feet.** If you've got crusty feet, take care of them. Foot care is not expensive and you can work on those dogs while watching television. No one wants to see dry and flaky feet. Yeah, you know who you are. Two words – pumice stone.
- **Ugly toenails.** If your nails aren't pretty, cover them up. There are plenty of closed-toed summer shoes. If you want to show your piggies, clean them, file them, polish them, love them. They are supposed to accentuate the shoe, not insult it. If your nails are yellow, see a doctor. That is not a natural color. If you are a man, don't think that you are off the hook. Polish is optional but all other rules apply.
- **Corns.** There's not much help for those with old corns but I'm sure there is a limit. If you are over the corn limit, think about sandals that cover most of your toes and let the tips peak out. If you've embraced your corns, at least file them down and minimize them as much as you can.
- **Evil Stink.** If your feet stink get rid of your shoes. No matter how much you wash (and hopefully you're scrubbing those babies at least once a day), your feet are only as good as the shoes they are in. Keeping your feet dry and cool are a good way to avoid the stink.
- **Shoe care.** Change your shoes. If you only own two pair of shoes, you are good to go. Your shoes need a 24-hour

rest period, otherwise they become a breeding growth for fungus and funk. Teach your kids while they are young that this is an important rule. Dry shoes and dry feet (not ashy) foster good pediatric health.
- **Foot hair.** If you've got foot hair and everybody can see it you need to turn yourself in to the nearest authorities. The fashion police have been looking for you. Foot hair is embarrassing and gross. You can take care of that the same way you take care of all unwanted hair. Shave them, bleach them, pull them out one by one. Just get rid of them.

No one expects you to have a perfect pair of feet. But, if from a distance of five or six feet yours are frightful, you need to work on them a little. No one should have to look at your ugly feet.

Be careful who your friends are

I've got a friend who is overweight. When we get together, she gives me the lowdown on her fat life – what she ate, what she didn't, how much she lost/gained. You get the idea. It's very tedious.

I've got a friend who is single. When we get together, she laments about the single life. She updates me on who she's dating, who she just broke up/went out with. She tells me her pie-in-the sky dream fantasies about what her life would be like if she wasn't a Onesie. Sometimes I think she makes some of it up.

I've got a friend who is always broke. She never has a spare dime and feels like she has to give me her financial portfolio every minute of every day. Honestly, I've got my own money problems. I don't want to hear about her's.

I've got a friend whose husband is a bum. I don't know if he's really a bum so much as every time she has something to say about him it puts him in a negative light. I used to suggest that she dump him, but now I know that she won't. She'll just keep talking about what a bum he is.

These are my downer friends. Those who like to wallow in the misery they create and would be ecstatic for me to join them, are downers. I used to think that they just needed a pick-me-up, but they don't. Downer friends like to be down. These are the friends I could stand to lose.

I've got a friend who is successful. She overcame statistics, odds and obstacles to get where she is today. She talks about her dreams in a way that you know she'll achieve them. You just know from listening that the world is hers for the taking. I love just listening to her talk and I get the feeling I should always carry a notebook when she's around.

I've got a friend who is smarter than me. Whenever I talk to her, I have to think hard to keep up. I poke fun at her for using highbrow words, but the truth is it's refreshing to have to check a dictionary when she's not in the room.

I've got a friend who is happy. Not every day, but in the larger contented sense. She fusses with her husband and she could stand to lose a few pounds, but you'd never guess by talking to her. She is a joy to be around and whenever I'm with her I have to force myself to go home.

I've got a friend whose sole purpose in life is to be an example for other Christians to follow. Every word and action is in true consideration of Christ. She is the only person I know that is a daughter of God in every sense. She is light in a dark room and radiates on others around her.

These are my upper friends. They are out in the world doing things. They aren't perfect. They aren't special. But, they get up, dust themselves off and do things that make a difference. They find something good in every situation. In the face of adversity, they find strength in themselves. These are the friends I treasure.

Life is short. Choose your friends wisely. Shake off your downer friends. They are just bringing you down. Surround yourself with friends who positively impact your outlook on life.

Dear Future Me,

I sent a letter to myself. I expect it to arrive on my 50th birthday – August 20, 2020. Providing, of course that I (1) am still alive, (2) still have the same e-mail address, and (3) don't assume it is spam and delete the message.

I asked myself if I was happy. This is the sort of thing you want to be sure of in the future. Theoretically, if you are not happy in your 30s, you're aggressively working on positive changes. So the big question is did my hard work pay off?

I asked myself if I'd gotten my master's degree. "Education is the key to choices," I reminded my future self. My 30s have been dedicated to educating myself so I'm pretty certain that 50-year-old me is going to have a lot more career options than I do today. Especially, if I stick to my education plans.

I asked how my daughter was doing. Did she become a vet? Today, all she talks about is working with animals. But, of course, at her age I wanted to be a journalist. Oh, wait, bad example. What I mean to say is kids change their minds one million times before they finish college, so what did my daughter wind up doing with her life?

I asked myself how my family was. Were the sisters and their families healthy and happy? Was my mom doing okay? I didn't ask about my grandmother. I should have. She could still be alive and in her mid-90s. I certainly hope she is.

I asked myself if I'd learned to manage my weight. That's a big issue for me. I don't want to be 250 pounds or larger when I'm 50. I asked whether or not I'd been successful at making a change.

I sent prayers to myself for my family and the world in general. I'm not sure what the rules are about asking God to bless the future you, but I gave it a try.

I made a list of technology that my generation loves. Will there still be CDs, DVDs, iPods, microwaves and PCs?

What will the state of the world be? Will we have the same allies and enemies? Will we be at war or peace?

I closed my email with "I love you." I wanted my future self to know that she was loved – past, present and future.

If you could send a letter to your future self, what would you say? To try it, go to www.futureme.org.

Albums that changed my life

Rolling Stones magazine recently published a list of 40 Songs That Changed the World. The list includes Purple Haze, Dancing in the Streets and That's Alright.

I agree with some of the songs on the list. Bohemian Rhapsody, Walk This Way, When Doves Cry are all worthy to have made the list. I don't agree with Blitzkrieg Bop (huh?), I Feel Love or Baby One More Time. But, hey, it's not my list.

I was inspired to write my own list. Instead of narrowing it down to songs, I decided to make it of albums or CDs that changed my life. Here it goes:

Alanis Morissette's Jagged Little Pill. I was in my early 20s. I was all about angst and alternative music back then.

Solo debut album**, Introducing the Hardline According to Terence Trent D'Arby**. His sound was very raw, acoustic and gravelly. This album was released during the early days of MTV's Unplugged when esoteric music was en vogue. I was in Europe redefining myself when this CD came out. I thought it was very Euro chic to listen to music that bucked that techno 80s sound.

John Lennon and Yoko Ono's Double Fantasy. This shows my mother's influence on my music choices. When we did housework on Saturdays, Mom played one of three choices – Beethoven, Tchaikovsky or John Lennon. I liked Lennon the best. Whenever I hear songs from this album, I'm tempted to clean. Beautiful Boy and (Just Like) Starting Over are the best. There's some wacky Yoko stuff on the album, but otherwise it's brilliant. It was his last album, released weeks before his death.

Phoebe Snow's Never Letting Go. This is another of my mother's old favorites. It was released when I was five years old. Even at that age, I knew all the words to all the songs. Snow's album is bluesy and jazzy and full of feminine spirit. Snow reminds me of my best childhood memories from a time when I loved my mother unconditionally.

Brandy's Full Moon. I've always been a fan, but this one is her coming of age recording. She has a sultry voice that belies her age. Songs on this CD transport me to a different place. I was new to Texas when this CD was released. I had left my own life and struck out on my own – it was a coming of age time for me to.

Shania Twain's Come On Over. This was the first 'country' music CD that I had the guts to buy. I was afraid that country was not cool. I had to fight the stereotype that black people only listen to hip hop, R&B and soul. Even though I'd always secretly been a fan of Patsy Kline for years, I'd only casually browsed *that* section of the store until this CD came along and I gathered up the courage to buy it. Some will argue that Twain is more pop than country, but if her music can bring someone like me into the genre, more success to her and the industry.

Garth Brook's No Fences. I stole this CD from an ex-boyfriend. This is Brook's greatest CD ever, as far as I'm concerned. There are no throwaways on this one. It's all music. I love eight of the 10 songs, which include Friends in Low Places and Mr. Blue, and my favorites Unanswered Prayers, The Thunder Rolls and Wild Horses. This CD picks me up when I'm down and reminds me of its previous owner.

Natalie Cole's Inseparable. She took a lot of criticism for this album, but the duets with her father are remarkable and her voice and style are at their peak. I have been a fan of hers since I was born. If my life were a musical, Cole's music would be the soundtrack.

Forrest Gump: The Soundtrack is one of the greatest CDs of all times. There are two discs, so you know you are getting your money's worth. What I like most about this CD is its variety. There are a lot of artists featured and it spans four decades of classic American music.

REM's Automatic for the People was my introduction to the band and also opened me up to alternative music. There is a spirit in that album that begs you to take off your shoes and dance in a circle. This CD came out during a time when I was exploring my musical needs and moving out of rap and R&B and into what I thought was a more soulful indy acoustic and alternative rock. It came out during the original MTV Unplugged era.

Planet Rock by **Afrika Bambaataa and the Soulsonic Force** is the first rap song that I could sing word for word. Rap music, when it hit, was the most fantastic sound I'd ever heard. Even though I was about 11 years old, I was transformed by rap. Who wasn't?

Rapper's Delight by the **Sugar Hill Gang** also came out in the early 1980s. The record was cool and you could dance to it. The record was also affordable for a kid on a weekly allowance. Today, that music reminds me of what was good and idyllic about my childhood. At the time, my mother had packed up and joined the Army. Fond memories, from what was becoming an increasingly complicated life, were cherished.

Weird Al Yankovic's Bad Hair Day is, in my opinion, his best work ever. Okay, I know that makes me a geek. I've always been a fan of his. He is both talented and funny. Weird Al cleverly parodies popular songs. He writes his own material and you get the impression that he does this late at night in his mother's basement. Amish Paradise, a classic, is a parody of Gangster's Paradise.

Luck of the Draw by **Bonnie Raitt** is always my 'go to' CD when I need to release some stress. I frequently listen to it in the car where I can sing at the top of my lungs uninterrupted. If I am pensive, depressed, aggravated or mad, Bonnie is my girl. I actually wore out my CD. A friend of mine gave me his cassette. If it breaks, I'll go out and buy it again.

Kraftwerk's Trans-Europe Express. It is possible that my three sisters and I are the only people in this country who still remember the song 'Numbers' on this album. I spent years trying to figure out the name of this one and have yet to find a copy. When we moved to my grandfather's house, my step-grandmother bought this album. My three sisters and I loved it. We played it all the time.

At the time, we thought the language was Japanese, but still, we knew all the words. We made up dances and performed for company. I mean we really loved this album. More than a decade later, I realized that it was actually German and I could translate the lyrics that I knew so well.

Grammy CDs: I enjoy the CDs released by Grammy each year that features award nominees. What I like most is that all of the songs on each CD represent the best and most popular songs across the music spectrum. My life was not changed by these CDs, but I am definitely more entertained as a result of them. I eagerly look forward to the release of a new one each year.

Great Books I

When I was eight I had an accident that left me on bed rest for a few weeks. My mother decided this would be the perfect opportunity for summer reading.

She brought me a stack of novels from the library. This is my earliest recollection of literature. Here's what I read while I recovered in bed with one foot elevated:

- **Jonathan Livingston Seagull** by **Richard Bach**. Behind a story about a young seagull learning to fly is a journey of self-discovery. This is a fantastic story and age-appropriate for preteen boys and girls.
- **Roll of Thunder, Hear My Cry** by **Mildred D. Taylor**. A story about a Depression-era black, southern family brings to light the struggle over human condition. This is an award-winning children's literary novel.
- **Soul Sister** by **Grace Halsell**. A lot of my favorite books center on women and African-Americans. This is a result of my mother's influence. Soul Sister is about a white woman who disguises herself as a black woman to experience life from a different perspective.

In the same year, I read **Roots** by **Alex Haley**. Every American should read this book despite its massive size. It is not only a great story it is the most comprehensive, fact-based recollection of the condition of slavery in print. I've read it twice.

Sometime in my childhood, I read **The Chronicles of Narnia: The Lion, the Witch and the Wardrobe** by **C.S. Lewis**. I was transported to the most beautiful fantasy world ever created. I wanted to try Turkish Delight. My logic: if it's good enough to sell out your siblings for, it must be delicious.

I did not know, at the time, that this book was one in a series. It would be many years before I discovered the others. All in all, I've read the chronicles three times. I've enjoyed Turkish Delight. I haven't sold out my siblings yet.

I also read **Lord of the Rings** by **J.R. Tolkien**. It is another magical story; a little scarier than gentle Narnia. This is a complicated story but beautifully told. I love fantasy. I just recently read the entire trilogy.

Are You There God, It's Me Margaret? by **Judy Blume** was the first book that spoke to me. I didn't know you could make friends with characters until I read about Margaret. Blume defined the childhoods of millions of girls my age. Her books are reprinted for a new generation. I was very lucky to have grown up not far from Judy Blume's home so girls in my area discovered her long before the rest of the country.

In the eighth grade I read **Little Women** by **Louis May Alcott** and **Anne of Green Gables (not just one book)** by **Lucy Maud Montgomery**. Between Jo March and Anne Shirley, I drifted through my preteens with a nose in many books.

As a freshman in high school, I chose **Earnest Hemingway's A Farewell to Arms** for a book report. My English teacher, Miriam Feitel, was shocked and a little concerned about my choice, but I promised her I would get it read in enough time to make my deadline. I'm glad I chose it. I read it and experienced my first bout of depression. It is about love, war, loss and rain. It is an emotional roller coaster. I've since read it a second time.

Great Books II

"They shoot the white girl first. With the rest they can take their time. No need to hurry here." Oprah Winfrey recited the first few lines of **Toni Morrison's Paradise** at the onset of one of her shows about books. When I heard it I knew I had to read the book. Morrison, a Nobel prize winner, is a tough read. I had to immediately read it again to absorb it all but it was a white-knuckle tale about small town lies and deceit from beginning to end.

Here are more of my favorite books:

The Mists of Avalon by **Marion Zimmer Bradley** was given to me by a friend when I was in my 20s. It is the retelling of Arthur and Gwennhywfar from a mystical female perspective. It is a non-traditional story where familiar characters are bound together in unexpected ways.

I read **Memoirs of a Geisha** by **Arthur Golden** in one night. I was on a business trip and stayed up until 3 a.m. with this book. I couldn't put it down. I don't know what it is like to be a Geisha, but I believe it is exactly as Chiyo explained it.

I read **The Children of Henry VIII** by **Alison Weir** as an assignment in college. I love history. I love fiction. I love historical fiction. This one is based on real letters, records and documents but it reads like seedy fiction. I loved it. It was like poking around in royal boudoirs.

Circle of Friends by **Maeve Binchy** reminded me of the books I read as a child. The characters are people readers want to get to know. This is a storyteller's story. I went to Ireland years after I read the story and followed the footsteps of parts of the book. I wish I could say that Binchy is one of my favorite authors but she is not. I've not found another book that I've liked nearly as much as this one. I read Tara Road and The Quentins years later and really struggled through them. I couldn't find a single character that I liked and I found her writing style annoying. She is world-renowned and monetarily successful but I can't figure out what her appeal is.

Amy Tan's The Joy Luck Club is a favorite book of mine. Tan's mother-daughter conflicts transcend ethnicity. I also enjoyed The Bonesetter's Daughter. I mean to read more of her novels.

Connie Briscoe's A Long Way Home is about three generations of slave women in Virginia. I love to read anything Briscoe writes. She normally sticks to contemporary fiction. This one was a successful leap of faith on her part.

How far would I go for Turkish Delight?

I read **The Chronicles of Narnia: The Lion, the Witch and the Wardrobe** when I was about ten years old. I loved it. I didn't know that there were seven books in the series, but when I found out, I read those too. I've actually read the series three times so far. Now that my daughter's taken an interest in the books, I may just read them again.

In chapter four, Edmund, the youngest boy, meets the White Witch Jadis who tells him she is the Queen of Narnia. She gives him hot chocolate and several pounds of Turkish Delight. The treats are enchanted, having been made of magic by the evil snow queen. The more Edmund eats, the more he wants to eat. He gobbles up the sweets and stares greedily at the empty round box with the green silk ribbon.

When he asks for more and offers to accompany her back to the palace to get it, the queen tells Edmund that she'll crown him heir to the throne and give him rooms and rooms full of the best Turkish Delight if he'll return to her with his siblings – one Son of Adam and two Daughters of Eve. Edmund agrees and hatches a secret plan to lure Peter, Susan and Lucy to the witch's castle where, unbeknownst to him, she intends to kill them all.

At ten, I had no idea what Turkish Delight was. I had never heard of it or tasted it. But, I thought, it must be something spectacular if someone were willing to sell out his siblings to get his hands on some. I was an adult by the time I sampled Turkish Delight, and, my goodness, it was delicious! Though I didn't plot against my siblings to get more, I do look forward to this time of year when Turkish Delight is readily available.

Turkish Delight is a holiday tradition for my family. We usually buy it from Liberty Orchards, a Washington-based, family-owned company that started with two Armenian friends in the 1920s. They call their candies Applets and Cotlets, but the recipe is based on traditional Middle Eastern Rahat Locoum.

The best Turkish Delight has pistachios in it. Americanized recipes call for walnuts. Fruits can vary, but are always dried. Rosewater or lemon juices are added for fragrance. Lastly, Turkish Delight is always coated in white powder, a mixture of cornstarch and confectioner's sugar.

And what became of Edmund? Well, he did become a King of Narnia, but not because of the witch. He along with his brother and two sisters, ascended to the throne after a terrible battle with the witch and her evil army. Edmund fought valiantly and was known throughout the land as King Edmund the Just.

There are seven books in The Chronicles of Narnia series: The Magician's Nephew; The Lion, the Witch and the Wardrobe; The Horse and his Boy; Prince Caspian; The Voyage of the Dawn Treader; The Silver Chair; and The Last Battle.

Mean Girls

It all started when my daughter decided to have sushi with chopsticks for lunch. We had leftovers from the night before and that's what she decided to take to school. No harm in that, right?

My lunch instructions are simple. Must be well-balanced. Must contain two fruits or vegetables. Must be something that can be eaten cold. Sushi fits the bill.

My daughter must have thought it would be cool to show off her chopsticks skills to her classmates. Well they weren't impressed. They were decidedly unimpressed. The sushi decision made my daughter the object of ridicule.

For weeks, what she had for lunch was the topic of the day. Apparently there's a list of acceptable lunches that I don't know about. My kid was miserable.

At the center of the controversy was one girl. An eight-year-old.

Something about little girls turns them from sweet, eager-to-please kittens to nasty, evil little witches. It happens in about the third grade and continues until they die.

What forces the change? Hormones? Probably. But that seems like an easy answer to a complicated question.

Could it be the environment? Maybe. Don't you just hate those sass-talking brats on television shows that our daughters love to watch? Then there are movies like Mean Girls, Bring It On and The Cheetah Girls where even the good girls interact with each other in less than positive ways.

Girls also get their behavior cues from women. Are our daughters reflections of their mothers? You bet. They watch how we talk to store clerks, in-laws and our own mothers. They mimic our behavior because they think it's acceptable. And Lord knows we can be a nasty bunch.

Maybe this cattiness is a defense mechanism. Maybe little girls are insecure and lash out to protect themselves. Maybe girls are so afraid of being the object of unwanted attention that they deflect that attention before it turns on them.

My daughter is a victim in this, but she's not innocent. I've called her on the way she talks to her friends when she thinks I'm not listening. I've scolded her for her new habit of giving sassy, eye-rolling, tongue-clicking answers.

I don't know what makes her this way, but I'm afraid this is just the beginning. I've heard horror stories about daughters who used to be sugary sweet. I'm told my daughter's time is coming.

I don't know why girls, or women, tend to interact with each other in this demeaning manner. It's bad and wrong and destructive yet most of us are comfortable in the realm of meanness, cattiness and, oh, what is that other word?

But, back to school....

I don't know why this girl chose my daughter as her target. There is no amount of advice that I can give my daughter to improve this situation.

She, like a billion other girls, will have to find the strength to either rise above the situation or stand up to the girl.

I probably won't find out how this story ends. My daughter is going through a closed-mouth, sullen phase and doesn't share much. But that is a topic for another day.

Fashion faux pas

I absolutely hate to see people shop in what can only be described as pajamas. Oh, you know who I'm talking about. Those people who come to the store wearing oversized shirts, ratty sweats and slippers; carrying babies in diapers; and carting kids with no shoes.

So imagine my surprise when, dressed in sweat pants, a Mexican pullover and flip flops with socks, I was caught one night shopping.

There are certain trips to the store that a woman must make in the middle of the night. There are the 'Uh-oh, we are out of toilet paper,' 'What do you mean there's no cough syrup?' 'The %$@#!!!! toilet is backed-up again,' and the 'I must have ice cream or die.' In my case, it was the fourth, with cake. Thank goodness there are stores open 24 hours to fill that critical need.

I decided to go out as I was -- in my Saturday night wear. Getting dressed would have taken too much time. Besides, it was late. I figured I could slip in and out within five minutes. I didn't expect to run into anyone I knew at the store.

Wrong. For two reasons: (1) Murphy's Law states that when you look your worst you will run into every person you know, and (2) apparently, I am not the only person who shops in the middle of the night.

Not two seconds after I entered the store I ran into a family of friends. I gave them a curt smile and quick wave followed by a brisker walk. I put on the 'this is an emergency' face just in case they noticed that my socks in no way matched the rest of my outfit or anyone else's outfit for that matter.

As I returned from the ice cream aisle, I ran into a colleague. Of course, it wasn't the type of co-worker I could giggle with about my fashion faux pas over coffee on Monday. It was the put-together type of gal that made me, in that instant, feel like a schlump. Having been snagged twice, I figured it was time to get the hell out of the store.

How important is it to pay attention to what I'm wearing when shopping in the middle of the night? Am I trying to make a good impression at that hour?

Well, yeah. I am. I was more embarrassed at being seen than at being dressed like that in the first place. I should have taken the time to throw on some jeans and real shoes. I'm sure someone saw me and assumed I was one of those people. Knowing that kills me. I hate those people.

What's up with Smilin' Bob?

In the middle of watching Ground Hog Day, the movie starring Bill Murray as a weatherman forced to repeat Feb. 2 in Punxsutawney, Penn., a commercial for Enzyte came on. You know the one with Smilin' Bob, who keeps his wife in a pleasant mood and is friendly to all the neighbors' wives? Well the next thing that happened was my daughter asked, "Why is he so happy?"

Are you kidding me? Now I have to explain THAT?! What is that commercial doing coming on at 6:30 p.m.? I expect it at midnight, when it is accompanied by mindless infomercials and local hot chicks waiting for your call. That's why I don't let my daughter watch television at midnight. But, this was on a Saturday, deep in the middle of family time.

There was a time, years ago, when there were sacred cows in advertising. Sure, people smoked and drank in commercials, but you'd never have to worry about condoms or tampons. We knew that condoms and tampons existed and we knew where to get them, but we didn't have to watch them on television.

Today, there is nothing sacred. There's nothing left unsaid and drug advertisements are about the worst. I don't want to have to explain Levitra or Yaz. I don't want to tell my daughter what happened between Mr. and Mrs. Carey, with the KY Yours & Mine before the kids came home.

And then there are the bonehead commercials where sexuality is more prevalent than product sales. How about that beer commercial where the woman is an automated drink dispenser? I don't want to see a half-naked pop star soaked in bubbles peddling burgers or women wrapping themselves around a drainage pipe whose source is a shower where Axe products are being used. Actually, any product featuring scantily-clad women results in an immediate loss of this potential customer.

I'm not saying down with sexy commercials. I'm saying there is a time and a place – oh, I don't know, after 10 p.m. on cable channels, maybe? I don't think advertisers should make parenting even more difficult by putting this junk out there without any kind of warning. If my daughter were watching VH1 or the CW, I would understand the risk, but I don't allow her to watch those. And, if we are watching a family movie, we are in a PG zone.

It's not just the sexy commercials. I hate the stupid ones too. I hate any and all caveman commercials. They are just plain dumb. I can't believe that ad campaign has gone on for years. I hate Snapple and Quizno commercials. They are moronic and creepy. Those stalker mop and broom Swiffer commercials get on my nerves. I don't like commercials that portray men as sports-loving mouth breathers. I don't like commercials with sass-talking brats; goofy frat boys; 'hood rats; or women with big breasts and small brains. I don't like talking animal commercials (except for the Advantix one about the puppy who goes to summer camp). I hate Billy Mays and all his inventions, whether they are useful or not. He is whiny and annoying. And I don't like the shampoo commercial where the woman uses her hair as a paintbrush.

While on the subject of commercials, let me just say that I don't like those 'feed the hungry children' commercials. They don't make me want to write a check; they make me change the channel. And, if the producers put the money they spent on those commercials into the hands of the very people they are trying to help, they might actually make a difference in the lives of third world children.

Commercials should be fun or clever or interesting. I'm not looking for Addy-worthy campaigns, just evidence of brain usage. I love the Dove Real Beauty campaign. I actually switched to Dove soap in support of the message that all women are beautiful and none are perfect behind their products.

I love the Johnson & Johnson commercial where the mom says she never expected to short and bald to be so cute and the one where the dad stays home from his poker game to play with his kids. I love greeting card commercials and the ones about kids going off to college. I really like the 'Go Meat' commercials.

And now, as I am finishing up this column and my daughter is in the other room watching Night at the Museum, Smilin' Bob has struck again. Natural Male Enhancement has made Bob the hit of the holiday party. Here we go again....

How old is too old to drive? I don't know

I was driving behind an elderly woman the other day. We stopped in the turning lane at a red light. When the light turned green, she immediately turned left, ignoring the vehicle coming from the opposite direction. There was almost an accident.

When I turned, I pulled up behind her, then moved into the right lane to turn. She remained in the center lane, but turned. Lucky for me, I was already wary of her driving abilities. I hit my brakes and let her turn.

She reached a large parking lot and drove straight across it with no regard to lanes or spaces. She struggled a bit to get out of the car. I noticed that she was barely five feet and white-haired. She was a little stooped and did not walk with ease. She was old.

At first, I was angry with her. People like her ought to stay off the %&*#! road. But then I thought, it must be difficult to give up your license.

Having a car comes with a level of freedom. Not having to depend on others, being able to go whenever and wherever you want are freedoms only possible with your own set of wheels. There is also the psychological boost of being independent and competent.

I used to think that the government should summarily take your license away on your 65th birthday. *Good afternoon, Mr. Jones. We heard today is your birthday. Hand over your license and nobody gets hurt, old man.*

I don't think that way anymore. I know too many people, my 70-something grandmother included, who are perfectly fit to drive. I do think it is not unreasonable to test seniors every year.

What would be more effective is for people to accept that they are no longer fit to drive and hand over their licenses voluntarily. But, I have no idea of what it might be like to admit that I am no longer able to take responsibility for this aspect of my life. It seems that I'd really have to swallow my pride to make that confession. I don't know if I could do that so I don't think it is fair to expect someone else to.

So what is the next option? A friend of mine went out and disabled her mother's car whenever the old lady threatened to get her keys. That proved to be effective for a while, but ultimately it came to a showdown between mother and daughter and mom lost her keys, her license and a little of her dignity. How old is too old to drive? I have no idea.

A look into past lives

Did you ever notice that when people speak about their past lives they were always of some distinction? People recall being passengers on the Titanic or a Roman soldier or the Queen of England. People tell you that they fell during the Battle of Bunker Hill or was the trusted counselor of a great pharaoh.

Nobody, except Albert Brooks in the movie Defending Your Life (a great movie), can recall being something like a chamber maid, a grave digger or that guy who follows the parade with a shovel.

Brooks' character in the movie got to look at his past lives and found that he was a lion's lunch. Meryl Streep found that she was Prince Valiant and Joan of Arc. Yeah, sure she was.

I've given past lives a fair amount of thought over the years. I'm still not sure if I believe we get to come back but it is a romantic notion.

I don't think I'd mind coming back as someone else. I like the idea of second chances. I'd want to get some things right. I'd like to be better and smarter. I'd like to be kinder, more loving and more forgiving. I'd like to have a more secure relationship with God.

Some believe that not only do you get to come back but you improve your lot in life according to your good deeds. I don't think I like the idea of suffering for something I don't remember doing. That is the ultimate form of punishment. I can't imagine going through life being good for the sake of my future life. But isn't that the basis of Christianity, in a way? To be good in this life and rewarded in heaven? And, the Bible says that we suffer the sins of our ancestors, so I think I'm bound to suffer no matter what.

I don't know what past lives I've had, if any. I can imagine I was a British soldier who fell in the Forest of Argonne or a Native American princess who brought together great tribes or an African warlord who ruled the Ivory Coast. Or maybe I was the guy who followed the parade with a shovel.

Is she or isn't she?

I have a colleague who I suspect is pregnant. I mean I really suspect she is pregnant. But, I'm going to wait until she says so first.

Years ago, I stopped a woman in the store. She was my sister's friend who I'd only met a couple of times. She had two small daughters and appeared, to me, to be pregnant a third time.

As it turned out, she was not. And, she was very, very, very angry with me. She lit into me right there in the middle of a department store. I believe I was even more embarrassed at being yelled at than she was at having been mistaken for pregnant.

The lesson from that incident was to never assume someone is pregnant. I don't care how pokey a woman looks or how much her girth has expanded since the last time I saw her, I will not assume that she is pregnant. Talk about the elephant in the room!

So, this puts me at a disadvantage with other women. Some will come up and say, 'Guess what?! I'm expecting!' and others will say nothing, waiting for me to notice first. And if I suspect, I'm not saying.

I don't know what the etiquette is for announcing a pregnancy. The way I did it back in 1997 was unique. I was in a conversation with a group of women at work. Someone mentioned that another woman was pregnant. A friend of mine, who I'd known for about a decade, wondered out loud when I was going to have a baby. I told her in November.

Well, she stared at me with her mouth wide open. It didn't take long for the news to spread. I was more than four months before I told anyone outside of my family. I didn't feel like making a big announcement. I wanted to keep it to myself for a while. As it turned out, there were nine women at my job pregnant at the same time. It was a fun time.

Maybe the woman I suspect is now pregnant doesn't want to make a big announcement. Maybe she's waiting for me to ask about it. Maybe she assumes I already know. Maybe she's not even pregnant.

Either way, I'm not saying anything.

A boy named Sassy

I have a cat. When I got him – he was just a kitten – I was told that he was a girl. I took the previous owner on her word. My daughter named the kitten Sassy.

After a few months, I took the cat to the vet to be spayed. The news from the doctor was shocking. My cat was a male. Turns out he was born that way.

I had him neutered and after a few hours brought him home. I broke the news to my daughter.

The dilemma was what to call him. Sassy is a decidedly feminine name, though based on his recent surgery gender was a moot point. We decided to butch up his name to Assassinator.

The problem is he really hasn't lived up to that name yet. He is about two-and-a-half and is the laziest, most timid specimen I've ever come across.

He spends most of his time outside and usually he can be found at the top of a tree hiding from a gang of feral cats who mean to kick his pampered ass. His little ears are scarred where other cats have torn into them, but we can't convince him to stay indoors.

When he spends time inside, he usually sleeps or licks himself. On many occasions, he licks himself until he falls asleep. It's very entertaining.

Surprisingly, our Sassy has outlived all of our other cats. Our beautiful and mean Phoenix could take care of herself but had a (fatal) habit of sleeping in the middle of the street. Snow Acre, who adopted us after we rescued her from a neighbor's tree was a street cat. Cheesecake, who even as a kitten used to smack poor Sassy around, was savvy and streetwise. Clarabelle found her way to my door and refused to leave. She was feisty enough to stand up to the dog. They are all dead now, mostly having fallen victim to cars or disappeared.

But, oh my Sassy. He brings joy to my life. I envy the simplicity of his. He doesn't ask for much. He only asks to be let in and out as required and he wants to be petted on demand. He likes to have his food bowl filled at all times. He wants permission to sleep on my bed and when he doesn't get it, he waits until I am asleep and climbs in 'til morning.

My cat. My sweetheart. My boy named Sassy.

My cat sneaks out the back door

My cat is cheating on me. I've had my suspicions, but when I saw him walking down my neighbor's steps, I knew. There was no hiding it.

The signs were there but I chose to ignore them. He doesn't spend a lot of time at home anymore. He doesn't stay; he just eats and leaves. When he walks in, he complains. I don't get his meal served fast enough. I don't pay enough attention to him. I don't give him what he needs. He had become very demanding.

Lately, we've argued quite a bit and I've yelled a lot. I knew we were having problems, but I thought we could work them out. I thought this was just a rough patch. All families go through them, right? I never suspected he would find another owner.

As I was driving home the other day, I saw him. At first, I thought it wasn't him. Why would it be him? I figured it was just some cat that looked like him. I know there is another cat in my neighborhood that looks like him from a distance. I told myself it might be that cat, not mine.

I ran across the street and called his name, certain he wouldn't answer. But he looked up at me and I knew. I was wrong. It was my cat all right. He just stood there, not even ashamed of himself.

I was hurt and angry. When I confronted him about it, he just sat down in the grass like he owned the place. He didn't have an explanation. He didn't say anything. Not so much as a 'meow.'

I've had my cat since he was about six weeks old. He is five now. When we moved to this neighborhood, he had to fight his way to dominance on our block which is overrun with tough street cats. He spends a large portion of the day on my roof or perched in a tree in front of the house, keeping up with the four-legged traffic.

I decided to confront the family. I rang the bell and when the door opened my neighbor said he didn't know who the cat belonged to. His wife had been feeding my cat and the one that looks like him. My cat hadn't told them about me. He'd convinced them that he was a stray.

Now I know why he refuses to wear a collar. I thought collars were uncomfortable but he just doesn't want people to know about us.

This changes our relationship and I don't know if I can go back to the way things used to be. I can't pretend this didn't happen. Every time I feed him, I'll wonder if he's already eaten over there. Every time

I drive by their home, I'll wonder if he is there. Every time I call and he doesn't answer, I'll wonder if he is out looking for another family.

My cheating cat has broken my heart.

Science and math for girls

I went to space camp recently. I had a blast! Pun intended.

My daughter and I joined hundreds of Girl Scouts from across Texas for an overnight stay at Johnson Space Center.

We spent the evening doing projects that promote math and science careers for girls. We explored astronomy, engineering, geometry, problem solving and leadership. We spent the next day touring the compound and the museum. We took a tour of the training modules modeled and sat in the historical viewing room next to where NASA engineers guided Apollo 13 astronauts back to Earth.

When presented in a manner that is fun and hands-on, science and math are fun. My daughter loves math and science. I want to preserve her fascination and excitement.

Someone said that science and math, which both require time and dedication, take a back seat in school when girls discover an interest in boys. I also heard that girls don't want to appear to be nerdy or brainy by excelling in the sciences. I've read that girls don't have the aptitude for advanced math. I know that girls are not always encouraged to work toward careers in science and math.

These are the stereotypes and assumptions I will have to combat over the next few years. I've got my eye on possible obstacles.

The first is myself. I don't like math and I often find science dull. I didn't excel at either. I failed Calculus twice in college and cried my way through Anatomy class. When dealing with my daughter, I try to keep my opinions to myself.

I try to expose her to women who are successful at technical, scientific and mathematical careers. The space camp was a great opportunity for her to see that there are many women astronauts and they all loved science and math as children.

I let my daughter do experiments at home. She has a telescope and a microscope. She is currently growing a crop of potatoes, herbs and flowers with varying results.

Another obstacle is school. I have to keep her engaged and support her during homework, projects and science fairs. I have to stay on her teachers to make sure she is given every opportunity to excel and take part in the things that interest her. I have to make sure that she is not discouraged even when she's not doing as well as others. I also want to make sure that her math and science teachers are qualified and absolutely love what they teach.

There are programs for high schoolers to take part in clubs, camps and other areas where science and math are discussed. I plan to get her involved in those. I want her to meet girls her age who share her interests, so they can uplift each other.

I don't know if my plan will work. I'll have to get back to you in 20 years. At that time, I hope to point to a picture on the wall at Johnson Space Center and say, 'See that astronaut? She's my daughter.'

Fit is fine, but skinny is scary

I was watching the news the other day and apparently models are too skinny. *Well, there's a news flash for you.*

A reporter interviewed two young girls. One was 5'9" and 110 lbs. The other was shorter and skinnier. The big one said she was perfectly healthy but her doctor wanted her to gain a little more weight. She called her physical proportions a freak of nature. To be so tall and so thin is perfectly normal for her. *Yeah, right.* The little one said that people should stop focusing on those who are too skinny and start focusing on those who are too fat. Especially children.

While I agree with her in theory, I still think she is a bonehead. And by bonehead, I mean she couldn't have been more than 90 pounds. Childhood obesity is a problem. Kids are more sedentary than ever. Parents are too quick to turn to fast food which can be purchased and eaten in the car. Sodas and unhealthy snacks are available to kids at school. Junk food commercials overwhelm kids with irresponsible eating options. It's not safe to let kids play outside without supervision. Fat, lazy parents breed fat, lazy kids.

But being too skinny is equally a problem. Kids use a diet soft drink as a meal replacement. Purging and extreme dieting become lifelong weight loss plans. Kids are given unrealistic expectations about their body weight. Kids equate thin with healthy so the thinner they are the healthier they are. Parents criticize kids for eating too much. The inundation of outside influences only exasperates the problem. Every time someone tells our kids that skinny is the only way to be, our kids either increase their efforts to be skinny or work harder to stay skinny.

As parents we can't get into our kids' heads to find out how they feel about their weight. Even with our best efforts most of us don't come near combating peer pressure. Some don't even realize there is a problem until a doctor becomes involved. Some of our children are so screwed up about their weight they are almost beyond our reach.

The problem with skinny models is that it chalks points up for the bad guys. The ones who expect us to accept this skinniness as a standard of beauty though most of us will never achieve it. When the standard weight is lowered, we unquestioningly accept that too. Our acceptance is equal to encouragement. Especially in the eyes of our children who don't readily see the negative aspects of extreme skinniness.

Emaciated boneheads perpetuate the stereotype that skinny means successful and beautiful. If you are skinny, you can be a movie star. If you are skinny, you can be a super model. If you are skinny, you can be happy.

Fit is an achievable goal for most kids. Kids can eat right and make healthy choices to be fit. Kids can be active in sports to be fit. Parents can encourage a healthy lifestyle and good body image. Parents can combat outside influences by giving kids real role models of all sizes.

My take on spankings

When my daughter was just a year old, I hit her so hard that I left my handprint on her arm. It was a split second incident in a situation of eminent danger, but I instantly knew it was very wrong. Even today, I can't accurately express how bad I still feel that I'd done that.

When I was a child my mother used to beat me with whatever she had in her hand. Mostly it was extension cords and hangers. Once, she smacked my face so hard I fell to the floor. I had complained about having to scrub a pot of burnt corn. I doubt I was ten years old. I was being a brat, but no child ever deserves to be slapped across the face. I knew as a parent that I didn't want to raise my child like that.

My grandfather, who I lived with after my mother left, never raised a hand or voice to any of us. He was a quiet man. If we got into his crosshairs, we'd get a calm talking to that hurt worse than any physical punishment. He was a model disciplinarian.

My step-grandmother, on the other hand, beat us out of anger and frustration. I recall cowering in a closet protecting my head from the blows of a wooden cane. Eventually, I learned to outrun her. She was an invalid and if you could get downstairs, you could get away.

I believe that children need to be spanked on occasion. Of course, there is a substantial difference between a spanking and a beating. A spanking doesn't leave welts. A spanking doesn't land a kid in a hospital or morgue. A spanking is an open-handed swat on the bottom. A spanking is not done with props.

When my daughter was three, I spanked her regularly. Now, at nine, she hardly gets spanked at all. At the age where we can discuss transgressions and punishments, spanking seems useless except in extreme situations.

I think if spanking is a primary form of punishment for kids, it has to get more severe as the child gets older to be effective. In my opinion, by the time a child is 12, you have to hit her over the head with a brick to get her to mind. And what does that solve?

So, I've evolved. There are few spankings in my house but I do not begrudge others who find spanking acceptable.

But there's the other side to it. We tend to blame parents for the actions of their children. We look at teenagers who are completely out of control, or engaged in criminal behavior, and say it's the parents fault for a lack of discipline. We can't have it both ways.

People have such strong opinions about hitting children. I wonder if people differentiate between spankings and beatings or if people are comfortable with absolutes. All sides have valid points and I don't think either side is completely right or wrong. I can only do what is right for my family.

Get to know me for me

Someone says to me, at least once a day, 'You look like someone I know.'

I am a pretty even-tempered person, but this sends me right over the edge. It offends me and I don't offend easily. Actually, *offends* is a soft word; it pisses me off.

There are two things about, 'You look like someone I know' that burn me. First, I wonder if my face is so uninteresting and unmemorable that I can morph into a million other people at a moment's notice. What about my facial features are so common that I am so easily mistaken for someone else? Is it the two eyes?

Second, obviously the person speaking doesn't care to get to know either me or the person I remind her of. What about the person I remind her of makes that person memorable enough to vaguely recall the face but forgetful enough not to bother to remember that person's name or what she really looks like. Is that person as uninteresting as me? Is that person not worthy of the time it takes to recognize on a second meeting? Is that person someone not worth getting to know? Am I someone not worth getting to know?

Obviously, the person I remind her of is neither a friend nor an acquaintance. The person I remind her of is probably just a nameless face in the crowd. So, does she really know that person? If she doesn't, how can I remind her of someone she really doesn't know?

If I see someone who reminds me of someone I know, I'll say, 'Have we met before?' We'll talk about where we may have met, what groups we belong to and tally up the people we know. In the process, we'll get to know each other. We may not become friends, we may not ever see each other, but we'll really get to know each other. On the off-chance that we do meet again, I hope you don't say, 'You look like someone I know.'

Shopping at 5 a.m.

When two things on your Christmas gift list appear on the sales circular for the Black Friday Blowout Sale at your neighborhood super store, you just have to drag your ass out of bed at 4:45 a.m. and join the crowd. And that is what I did one day after Thanksgiving.

First, let me say that I do not like to shop on the day after Thanksgiving. My motto is: I'll pay full price if it means I'll avoid the crowds. So, I'd never done the mega-sale thing before.

Second, let me say that I wasn't at home. I spent the holidays at my big sister's house in Killeen. But, you know, all super stores are more or less the same. So, when I saw some sought-after items on sale, I knew what I had to do.

I got off the couch, brushed my teeth, slipped on a pair of jeans and headed out the door. I got about three blocks away before I realized that I'd forgotten my wallet. No point in shopping without the means to pay, right? I turned around, went back in the house, and was back on the road in a matter of minutes.

When I got to the super store, I found the parking lot almost full. I was flabbergasted. You would not believe how far I had to walk to get to the store entrance from where I parked. I didn't actually believe that millions of people all over the country get out of bed at oh-dark-thirty once a year to take advantage of this highly-commercialized sales event. I thought only weirdos did this sort of thing.

The store was pretty well packed and well stocked. Consumers were bright and alert. They had maps of the store.

On my search, I had to navigate my cart around many obstacles but I did okay. I found my first item very quickly. I couldn't find the second item, though. I asked for help, but the store clerk sent me on a wild goose chase. It was five in the morning and she had to work, so I understood.

I never did find that second item. I just stood there in the middle of the aisle waiting for someone to offer assistance. No store clerk came to my aid, but a customer, deciding that she didn't want the item, pulled it out of her cart and offered it to me. What luck, huh?!

So, I had the two things I came for. It was still early, so I decided to do a little more shopping. I bought a game and a toy for my daughter. I bought a drill and a wreath for myself. None of these items were on sale, but they were reasonably priced.

I was in a good mood, having long forgot that it was nowhere close to daylight.

I figured the lines would be unmanageable, so instead of heading to the front of the store, I went through the garden center. Wouldn't you know it? I was the only one in line. I engaged in a little holiday banter with the cashier. I was in a good mood and I was done.

I grabbed my purchases, loaded the car and headed back to my sister's house. I checked back in at 5:45 a.m. Not bad.

I shrugged off my jacket, slipped off my shoes and burrowed under the covers on my sister's couch. I closed my eyes and after a few minutes realized that I couldn't fall back to sleep. Damn Black Friday!

Great gifts for holiday shoppers

If you want to read to your toddler in Latin in the vain hope that it will secure his future as a doctor or lawyer even though you are neither a doctor, a lawyer nor a Latin scholar, Bolchazy & Carducci Publishers, Inc. has some childhood favorites like *Cattus Petasatus: The Cat in the Hat in Latin* and Shel Silberstein's *Arbor Alma/The Giving Tree in Latin*.

If there's a history buff in your life, John Stewart's *America* is the gift to get. The most serious readers will guffaw at the incredible goofs, gaffs and all-out mockery of every truth we hold self-evident. And who says it isn't better the second time around? The newly released teacher's edition, a re-issue of the 2004 comedy classic, will bring tears to your eyes and milk out of your nose.

If you are a man of action, you'll want to join the fight for an Xbox 360. The hype and media frenzy has consumers thinking this is the greatest gift since Tickle Me Elmo. To add to the excitement, there are only about 50 units available for purchase before Christmas. Can you say toy store steel cage grudge match royale? Yeah, baby. Bring it on!

For the fairer sex, Danielle Steele launched a new smell this year. If the lady in your life didn't care to smell like J-Lo, Britney Spears, Elizabeth Taylor or Usher, here's one more celebrity scent to try. Or you could just buy a Danielle Steele novel. It doesn't really matter which one. Like celebrity perfumes, they are all pretty much the same. Here's a Deal or No Deal. Ten minutes after the launch of this season's most phenomenal game show, NBC made a marketing mad dash to stores with a board game and DVD version. If you want to experience winning a million without actually winning any money, this is the gift for you. If you just want your own home version of the new hot Howie Mandel, the DVD is your best buy. *Hi, Howie!*

Do you have a finicky feline? A particular parrot? An indecisive iguana? If you don't know what to buy that special pet in your life, try a gift card. Let Fido shop for his own favorite gift this year.

Only 16 more shopping days 'til Christmas. Happy Holidays!

The best and the worst gifts

Over the years I've gotten lots of fantastic Christmas gifts. I come from a big family so as a kid I hit the mother lode. My sisters and I didn't get expensive gifts. We seldom got 'the toy.' But, we got great toys, dolls and games.

My mother didn't want to raise girly girls so we never, ever got dolls and tea sets from her on Christmas. She also wanted to make sure that we were being educated, not just entertained. I lamented year after year about the Barbie dolls my friends got when I got dumb stuff like board games, magazine subscriptions and encyclopedia sets.

I got some good gifts as a kid. I remember getting a pair of metal roller skates from my uncle's girlfriend. I remember getting a Weeble Wobbles playground set when I was about four years old. I remember getting a paint set that used a squirt bottle and a spinning bowl. I'm sure I got a lot of other great gifts.

I also remember all the worse gifts.

I remember getting a Barbie beauty salon from my grandmother one year. It came with sinks that used real water, color tabs for hair and the works. When I opened the box and shook the contents on to the rug I noticed that some of the pieces were broken. When I tried to put it together, I found that there were parts missing. I gave it to my uncle but he couldn't put it together either. While my sisters played with their cool toys, I sulked.

My grandmother later exchanged the gift and I played with the salon for months, but I'll never forget how I felt Christmas morning.

When I was 19 my mother gave me a belt for Christmas. That's right. A belt. It was a nice belt but after all just a belt. I tried to put on a brave face as my sisters tore open boxes and boxes and boxes of toys, books, CDs, clothes and accessories. When my mother asked why I wasn't opening presents I gently told her I was done. And thanks for the belt.

Needless to say she was horrified. She'd forgotten to pick up the rest of my gifts. She'd put them on layaway. She'd gone back to pick up my sisters' presents but forgot mine. We went to the store later in the week and picked up my gifts and lots more, but I'll never forget the belt. And you know? I won't let my mother forget either.

While at a dinner party with an ex-boyfriend's family, he took my finger and measured it with a finger scale. We were all very excited about this and there was plenty of speculation about an engagement going around the table. Well, Christmas came and went and there was no ring. I don't remember what I got for Christmas that year but I distinctly remember what I didn't get.

Here's to the best and worst Christmas gifts! Happy Holidays!

Card games make handy stocking stuffers

While some families gather around the television this Christmas for a Wii tournament or an Xbox extravaganza, my daughter and I will pull out one of our favorite card games and play for hours. We love board games like Scrabble, Life and Cadoo, but nothing beats a no-tech, quick set-up card game.

My love of cards comes from my grandmother who was a heavy Pinochle player back in the 1970s. She also loved to sit on her bed and play Solitaire. We were allowed to watch her, but not speak to her. The only noise was the slapping of cards against each other. This was her alone time. Watching her quiet game was a privilege for me.

I grew up loving all kinds of card games and passed that love on to my daughter. I never did learn to play Bridge or Pinochle and I am only a novice Poker player, but there are some packaged games that I'm really good at.

Here are some stocking stuffer card games that your card-playing kids will love:

UNO: Classic and easy-to-follow game for up to 10 players. Our house rule #1 is to pick up cards until the player draws a usable one. House rule #2 is to stack Draw 2 cards until someone puts out a Draw 4 and make the next player draw the cumulative total.

Skip-Bo: The basic rules can make the game last 15 minutes or 50 minutes. The trick to winning is to stay focused on your stock pile. Don't be distracted by the cards in your hand even if you think you have a good hand. This game is for up to four players, but I've played in larger groups. It is easy to understand but takes practice to master.

Phase 10: This game takes a lot of concentration since players advance through the game at different levels and there is no easy way to keep track. It is a fun game and not hard to master. Six can play together.

4Mation: Another rummy-like game with runs and sets. Like *UNO*, *Skip-Bo* and *Phase 10*, the object is to be the first to get rid of all of your cards. This game, for up to six players, has power cards called Double-Cross, Revenge, Sabotage and Imposter. Up to six players can join this game.

FLUXX: The card game of card games. I was introduced to this game on a camping trip and spent the next six months trying to purchase it. Ultimately, I bought it from an online bookstore, but had some difficulty having it mailed since it has XX in the title (Imagine trying to convince the online sales agent that it is *not* porn). This game starts out with two basic rules – draw one card; play one card. Subsequently, it spirals completely out of control with changes to rules and goals. This game is for up to six players, but I've played in a much larger group. It is recommended for eight-year-olds and up, but I only recommend it for card game thrill seekers. It is absolute mayhem.

Adrian Jackson is a freelance writer in Beeville, Texas. Despite Nintendos, Play Stations, V-techs and that electronic monopoly game that runs with an ATM card, card games are still popular and continue to provide endless hours of handheld entertainment.

Christmastime is here

It's beginning to look a lot like Christmas.

I'm in a jolly Christmas mood this year. I don't know why. I don't generally get all wrapped up in the season like some people. I like Christmas as much as the next gal but there is a limit to my outward enthusiasm.

I've very excited about Christmas this year. Now that Halloween is over I can go public with my enthusiasm. I've already gone shopping for decorations, lights and Christmas gifts.

This is new territory for me. It used to annoy me that retailers shelve holiday matter shortly after school starts. I used to turn my nose up at people who rove the tree trimming aisles before Halloween. But not this year!

We have a moratorium on holiday music in my house. No Christmas songs from Dec. 26 through Nov. 1. That's the rule. Always has been. This year, my daughter had to rein *me* in on my own rule in September and October.

This is not my normal state of mind. When I was a child, we'd have custody fights over Christmas. Grandparents would argue over who we'd get to spend the holidays with.

As an adult, I still have those bad Christmas memories to mar my celebrations. I am sometimes depressed during this time of year, especially if I don't get to spend the holidays with family. But, for some reason, I got into the Christmas spirit very early this year.

We put up our tree on November 1. We actually put up three of our planned five trees. We've decorated one small tree so far. It is filled with white lights and red fake poinsettias. It's very elegant.

The large tree we put up hasn't been decorated yet. It has white lights. It is going to be our travel tree. It will have keychains and ornaments collected from all over the world.

The live tree that we will get when they go on sale, will be our homey tree with family pictures and ornaments my daughter made in kindergarten. That's the one I love the most. I like recalling the memories attached to each ornament.

Tree four is also a large one. It will have glass ornaments on it. I have a set of beautiful smoked glass antique-looking ornaments from Germany and a new set of red, purple and green glass ornaments from IKEA. I have to put this tree in my bedroom since I don't trust the kitten with it when I'm not home.

The fifth one is a small tabletop tree. I saw a decorating idea on television that I'd like to try. It was a tree filled with white pipe cleaner 'snowflakes.' It was gorgeous and I think it would be fun to put in the bathroom.

I can't wait to get it all put together. Maybe I'll invite you over to see all of my hard work.

Happy Holidays!

A cancer walk for Summer

Summer Jean went home last week. This may mean nothing to you but to others who have followed her battle with cancer since October, this means a great deal. It's cause for celebration and praise.

When I first laid eyes on Summer, she was in a photograph her Uncle Bobby brought to work. I remarked on her hair. She was born with shocking red hair and plenty of it.

Over the next few months, he gave us updates and showed off new pictures. Summer's hair went curly and she took on the bright-eyed look of a curious toddler. As people do, we marveled at how fast she'd grown.

Bobby complained about not spending enough time with her. Not long after her first birthday, he moved to be nearer to his family.

Summer, a few months shy of her second birthday, was diagnosed with acute myelogenous leukemia (AML). Her parents were still recovering from the birth of their second daughter just a few weeks earlier. They took her to Children's Medical Center. The news was devastating.

It would be unfair to even attempt to describe what they must have felt walking into that hospital with their baby. The tenth floor became a euphemism for cancer. It also became their home.

Friends and relatives put their own lives on hold to keep the household running smoothly during this crisis.

There was only a small amount of hope for Summer -- something like a 40 percent survival rate. Over the next few months, she endured treatments, therapy, illness, medicine, fevers, pokes, prods and her hair fell out. She had multiple rounds of chemo and every trip home was followed by weeks and weeks in the hospital. Those of us on the outside looking in were kept up to date by a web page regularly updated by a family member.

Summer became the darling of the tenth floor. The family made livelong friends, I'm sure. One nurse said she was sad to see Summer go but hoped never to see her on the tenth floor again.

Summer is home now. She can go about the business of growing up. Her seventh-month journey has come to a stop (not an end).

No one should ever have to go through what she and her family went through, yet, it happens every day. Cancer touches our lives at the most unexpected times. Cancer is so prevalent that we all know people who've survived cancer, succumbed to cancer, and those going through cancer treatments right now.

I'm glad to have been a witness in this victorious fight. I can't imagine the fear and helplessness Summer's parents must continue to feel every day.

I'll be walking around the high school track in the wee hours of Saturday morning. I'll be walking for a lot of people. One of those is Summer Jean.

Happy 106th Summer Jean

Hurray! Summer Jean hit the 100 mark recently. Not years – days. That is cause for celebration.

Summer is a three-year-old in Texas. She is the niece of a friend of mine. When she was a year old she was diagnosed with cancer. Her prognosis was not good. She was diagnosed with Leukemia and her chance of survival was frighteningly low.

Summer Jean immediately started chemo. She lost all of her curly red hair and celebrated her second birthday barely alert. She spent 160 days in the hospital. The treatments were successful and Summer Jean went home with her family to get on with her life. At the age of two, she became a local hero and a strong advocate for cancer research and awareness. She raised $6,000 for the Leukemia and Lymphoma Society. A block party was held in her honor and on the anniversary of her initial diagnosis, the mayor declared it Summer Jean Day.

She spent almost six months at home before she showed signs of illness. The only thing worse than being diagnosed with cancer is coming out of remission. Summer Jean returned to the hospital.

Knowing what to expect, Summer Jean was not the darling patient she had been earlier. She didn't like taking pills. She wanted to go home. She missed her baby sister. She hated having her hair removed. She just didn't want to be there. But through it all, she was a trooper. One month later she achieved a second remission but doctors suggested a different and more aggressive treatment – bone marrow transplant.

Basically, all of Summer Jean's blood was taken out and replaced with donor blood. Even her blood type changed. This was done on Jan. 4, 2008. It was not an easy process and recovery was long and slow. Summer Jean was ill, weak and had to be put into a medically-induced coma to aid in her recover.

Yet, she prevailed. After months and months of recovery, Summer Jean was able to go home with restrictions. Even at home there is a limit to the contact she and her family can have with the outside world. She is weak and struggling to walk again. She eats very little and sleeps a lot. She has missed out on many of the learning opportunities that are common for most three-year-olds but she is alive. Sometimes that is enough.

I cannot imagine what her parents have gone through these past few years. I can't speak with any kind of authority on what any parent in a similar situation goes through while their child is fighting for her life. But I can say that through it all, they have never lost sight of the power of God. They have remained faithful and prayerful on the darkest days as equally as on the brightest ones. They have summoned the mighty power of a prayer army to intercede on Summer Jean's behalf, every step of the way.

They are remarkable and though I've never met either of them, I consider them my friends. They have influenced the way that I look at the world and strengthened my belief that God's awesome-working power is here for us to witness every day. And when we are blessed enough to marvel at God's work, we can truly say that He is an awesome God.

Happy 106th, Summer Jean! And many, many more.

$5 for a toothbrush?

I bought a toothbrush the other day.

No matter how many toothbrushes I buy over the course of a year I am always shocked when I reach the oral hygiene aisle and am confronted by the cost of toothbrushes.

When I was a kid, you could get a decent toothbrush for 99 cents. Sometimes you could get one for 79 cents. Why now do toothbrushes cost as much as $5 each? Where are the people with the $5 smiles?

While purchasing a toothbrush I decided to check out mouthwash. Whoa! When did the price of mouthwash go up to $6? I bought the store brand which cost just over $2.50. Maybe my breath will be less fresh than it would have been had I bought the name brand. I don't know. I'll take my chances.

When I went to shop for fresh vegetables, I found that because of a low crop, consumers are asked to pay almost $3 a pound for tomatoes. I passed. I'll get my tomatoes in a can until the crisis is over.

Avocados have gone up too. When I was a kid, I couldn't tell an avocado from an armadillo, but now they want me to pay almost $2 for one?

I don't eat much meat anymore. Mostly, it's just too damned expensive. I spent over $3 on less than a pound of ground beef. That's my beef purchase for the month. Chicken is not much less expensive.

I drink soy milk. What I used to pay 99 cents for now costs $1.39. This is just in the last few months.

I wanted to buy sage since Thanksgiving is just around the corner. The cost? $3.99. Can you believe that? I sagely decided to leave it on the shelf.

When did prices go up so high? I thought a lot of it was blamed on the rising cost of fuel. Well gas prices have been going down. Why not food?

At what point do we stand up and say no? I'm not going to pay $8 for laundry detergent! I'm not going to pay $5 for a bag of nuts! I've had enough!

How much buying power does one consumer have? Can I start a grassroots campaign to drive down the price of lettuce?

Are you paying too much for your groceries? We should take to the streets. We should start a revolt. Who's with me?

Tooth Fairy

There is a menace lurking in our children's bedrooms at night.

Calling herself 'the Tooth Fairy,' this imposter will pay $5 for your child's tooth instead of the standard $1. This black market shyster will have you believe that $5 is the going rate for today's teeth when in all honesty she's squeezing small, mom and pop operations out of the market.

Don't be fooled into thinking that you have to compete by paying this exorbitant amount. You don't.

With all the sugar, salt and corn syrup kids chug down nowadays, teeth aren't the high quality they were 10 years ago. Most kids drink bottled water so there are not even the high levels of fluoride and chlorine there used to be.

When I was a kid, you got one quarter per tooth. If you were lucky two teeth would fall out at the same time and you got 50 cents.

The going rate was 25 cents and we were happy to get that. You could buy a bag of chips or a little brown sack filled with penny candy with that quarter.

The value of each tooth was equal to the cost of enough junk food to rot out the one next to it. That was a good rule of thumb.

There was nothing better than the feeling of a quarter under your pillow. If it was a shiny quarter, it was more valuable. You couldn't buy more, but you sure could show off more to your friends who got dull quarters. If it was shiny and bicentennial – well, it may well have been a gold coin for all it was worth.

So how did the price of a child's tooth get up to $5? I'll tell you how. It's those darn Joneses. Everybody is trying to keep up with them. I've never met these people, but they drive up the cost of teeth, Christmas toys and birthday parties just because they can.

The Joneses teach our kids that their teeth are so precious that they are worth a small fortune. We've got to put a stop to this nonsense.

We can do it if we all agree that a tooth is worth $1. But the minute one of us starts keeping up with the Joneses again, we're all sunk.

Dogs, trucks and bad things that happen

I hate to see dogs riding in the back of pick-up trucks.

Okay. Wait. Hear me out. I know that some are working dogs and that is the only way to get them around the ranch. I'm not talking about those dogs.

I'm talking about the ones in trucks speeding down Highway 181. I'm talking about the ones chained to the truck, the ones hanging over the sides, the ones left unsupervised in the back, and the worst of them -- the ones standing on top of the tool box in the flat bed cruising through the city.

I like dogs. I own a dog. I like him enough to let him occasionally ride in my car. I drove him to South Carolina and back.

My dog is not terribly bright. He's sweet, playful, loveable, boisterous, messy, loud and my heart would break if something were to happen to him. I've trained him to sit on the floor of the back seat of the car. He does it dutifully until I get out of the car. Then, he climbs into the front seat so he can look for me to return.

If I had a pickup truck, I don't imagine I'd let him ride in the back. There's room for him in the front. He's safer there anyway.

Every time I see a dog in a flat bed, I think about what would happen if the truck were in an accident. The dog chained to the truck would get strangled to death. The dog hanging over the side would get tossed over and pinned between the truck and a light pole. The dog unsupervised would jump out and run into oncoming traffic. The dog on top of the tool box would flip over the top of the truck, break through the windshield and kill himself and all the occupants in the truck.

My point is that it is not safe back there. If you love your dog, get him out of the back of that truck.

Be wary of strangers at the door

I want to apologize to the people who appeared on my front porch last Saturday. I bet they were from an area church but I didn't give them the time to explain.

It's not that I am a rude person. I try to be polite to strangers. I was raised to believe that everyone, regardless of who they are, deserves at least a minimum amount of respect. Some people say that you should always be nice to strangers at your door, because one of them could be an angel. My defense is that it is more likely that one of them is an ax murderer, a thief or a salesman.

My home is my sanctuary. It is the one place in the world that is truly my domain. My place is a haven from the outside world. I can do what I want, say what I want, and wear what I want in my home. I do not have to conform to societal impositions when I am in my space. I have very few visitors or guests and I like that just fine. I do not like strangers at my door because they invade my private space and time, and their presence forces me to take on a conventional role of hostess.

I have found that when strangers approach my door, they have a predictable purpose. They usually want to sell me something – magazines, candy or religion – and I'm not in the mood for buying. Strangers at the door are the original telemarketers. They pop up at the most inopportune moments. This most recent time occurred when I was on a long distance phone call with my sister.

Once on Halloween, a woman dressed in a costume came to sell cleaning products. I chided her, gave her some candy and told her not to come back.

Someone from an area church slipped a pamphlet in my door when I wouldn't let him in. The paper had the vilest and most offensive drawings I've ever seen in the name of Christianity. I threw it in the outside trash can. I would never bring that kind of evil into my home and it angered me that someone else would foist it on me.

A neighbor recently let some men in her home to use her phone and was robbed weeks later. I've heard that some strangers gain access to your home just to check out your valuables.

When I was a child, we had a screened porch that led to the door to the interior of the house. Strangers seemed to think that porch was put there for their comfort. They would let themselves in and sit on the rattan furniture until someone let them in. I always thought it rude and presumptuous of them to make themselves comfortable while we were held hostage inside tip-toeing around, peeking through a crack in the blinds to see if they were gone.

    I have a soft spot for some strangers. I offer water to the young Mormon men who make their rounds in my neighborhood. I know they don't drink coffee or soda, so something makes me think they never get enough to drink when they are out on their bikes all day. I don't let them in, having no interesting in becoming a Mormon but I give them a few bottles for the road.

    I am sometimes weak when kids show up to my door. Once, a teenager came in to sell me magazines that I didn't receive until six months later. I instantly regretted giving her a check because I've heard all kinds of horror stories about fraud and ID theft derived from giving a check to a stranger. It all worked out in the end, but I should have known when she said, 'I'm not here to force you to buy something,' that she was at least going to try.

Remembering the victim

Elora McKemy. That's the name I carry with me.

I tell people Elora's story whenever I can because whenever a shocking crime is committed the criminal lives in infamy while the victim is lost to time. The criminal is studied, written about, emulated and tracked. Long after he is gone, the glorification of his crime lives on.

His victim's life ended with her horrific death.

I never met Elora. What I know of her, I read in the paper or heard from people who knew her family. Here's her story:

The two-year-old was born in North Carolina. Her father was a soldier stationed in Babenhausen, Germany. Babenhausen, not far from where I used to live, is a rural city with a small U.S. Army base. One morning Elora's parents woke up and discovered that she was not in her bed. She was not in the house. She was nowhere to be found. It did not take long for the police to get involved in the disappearance. People immediately thought she'd wandered away. Some thought her parents were covering up a crime. By the time I went to work at 8 a.m., Elora's disappearance was all anyone could talk about.

Elora's naked body was found later that day in a ditch under a tree. She had been sexually assaulted and left for dead by a soldier who was acquainted with the family. To this day, no one knows how or why this happened.

It took German *polizei* and the U.S. military police a few days to piece together what happened, but they finally made the arrest.

I worked for Stars and Stripes at the time. Military police thought that the newspaper delivery driver might have some useful information about the crime. As it turned out he had unknowingly driven past the body hours after Elora's death.

When the case went to trial, in a military court, the perpetrator plead guilty. He said he was drunk that night, according to the newspaper. He said that he couldn't recall what happened but since the evidence pointed to him he must have committed the crime. That's all he said. He was sent to Fort Leavenworth, Kansas.

Elora's story was never told in court. There is only one person who knows exactly what happened to little Elora. He was the only witness to her pain and suffering and he never told what happened.

I won't tell you his name. I won't tell you on principle. I refuse to popularize the name of someone who committed such a heinous crime.

I choose, instead, to honor Elora McKemy who died September 15, 1993. I tell people her story so it is *never* forgotten, so she is never forgotten. Just keeping her name in my heart keeps her story alive.

Rest in Peace, little Elora McKemy.

Toddler dies by the hands of a monster

Elora McKemy didn't go off to college this year. She didn't graduate from high school. She never attended school. Her life was cut short in a gravel quarry on an Army base in Babenhausen, Germany on Sept. 15, 1993.

I was in Darmstadt at the time, living just a few miles away from where this story unfolded. Elora was taken from her parents' apartment in the middle of the night. She was raped, sodomized and left in a ditch to die by a soldier who was acquainted with her parents. He is now serving a life sentence in a military prison.

When it was discovered that the two-year-old wasn't in her bed, people immediately thought she'd wandered out of the apartment. Some figured that the door was left unlocked or maybe her parents were covering up a crime. The truth unfolded throughout the day in the most horrible and harrowing way. Elora had died a violent death at the hands of a sexual predator and monster. She was just a toddler and she died alone, naked on the ground.

When things like this happen parents like me feel powerless to make a difference. The act seems random and unfathomable to ignorant parents like me. We think that it could never happen to our children because we are vigilant about their safety. The truth is, we don't know child molesters and rapists on glance. You can't look at a person and tell. Many of us err on the side of extreme caution because we don't know who those people are or where they live or how they gain access to victims.

Texas Department of Public Safety posts a list of registered sex offenders which the general public can gain easy access to. There are 36 men on the Bee County list. They are sorted by name but each name links to an info page that gives readers a description, photo, status and list of sex offenses.

Of the 36 men on our list, only one was sentenced to serve more than 10 years. Not the one convicted of sexually assaulting a six-year-old boy or the one who sexually assaulted a three-year-old girl or the one convicted on incidents involving three different children. The man who got out early on a 20-year conviction had eight counts of indecency with a child involving sexual contact.

Some of the men on the list are unemployed but others work in the community. Some are contractors, some work for small companies and others work for large local businesses.

There are no women on the list but that doesn't mean that our children are safe from them. There have been some heinous acts of violence upon children perpetrated by women who, in general, are treated with much less severity if convicted than men.

I wish I could list the names of the 36 local sex offenders but I have to put my family's safety above that of the community at large. The list is fairly easy to access. It's on the DPS site. It's called 'Crime Record Service.' The web address is too long to list here.

Elora McKemy's mother died of brain cancer last May. She survived her daughter's murder. She survived giving birth to another child whom doctors told her she would never have. She survived divorce. And now she is with her little girl in a better place than I can imagine.

I tell people Elora's story so it is *never* forgotten, so she is never forgotten. Just keeping her name in my heart keeps her story alive. May it serve as a cautionary tale. We parents have to always be vigilant.

Rest in Peace, little Elora McKemy. Rest in Peace, Penny McKemy.

Adrian Jackson is a freelance writer in Beeville, Texas. Penelope McKemy died on May 17, 2009 in Hope Mills, North Carolina. Her ashes were sprinkled on Elora Nicole McKemy's gravesite at Fort Bragg Main Post Cemetery in North Carolina.

I occupied a black space

One common fear about having surgery is not knowing where you go. Where is that dark place that you reside in when you are unconscious? Is it like sleep? Is it suspended animation? Is it a temporary death?

I've had two surgeries and was 'put under' both times. I was nervous the first time. I was full of existential worries about what is what and where is where. I was concerned about my ability to find my way back from wherever it is we go when we are 'out.' I wondered if I'd wake up or, more importantly, if I didn't wake up where would I go. Would it stay black? Would I awaken abruptly in a new place and recognize that I'd been transported to Heaven (assuming that I am not going to Hell)? Would I be confused?

Dying during a surgery might be a very peaceful way to go but I think that not knowing the exact moment your spiritual self pulled away from your physical self would be mind-boggling. I think I'd like to know when I die. Or maybe I'd like to know when I'm definitively dead. I guess I don't really need to witness my last breath to know that I've moved on.

Millions of people have surgery everyday and don't die but they all occupy this black space that we don't understand. When I woke up from surgery in 2004 I was acutely aware of having been in the dark for an undetermined amount of time. Was I in a deep state of unconsciousness? Was I in a coma? I don't know what surgeons or anesthesiologists call that state that you are in during a surgery. Are you in limbo?

Being 'under' during surgery seems like being in limbo to me but limbo has negative connotations that make it less idyllic that it sounds to be. Where is limbo? Is limbo on the outskirts of Heaven or Hell? Is it simply oblivion or a place where lost things are?

Before I went into surgery the first time, I made a point of reminding myself to look at a clock to see how much time had elapsed during the procedure. I wanted to know how long I was out there in that place before I was called back to the present. As I was coming out of the fog, I remember making a point of looking at the clock on the wall of the recovery room briefly before slipping away again. To this day I cannot recall what time it actually was. What good did remembering to look at the clock do me? None, but it gave me a mile marker on the comeback trail. I knew that I was back even though I was not quite in full control of myself.

I am blessed to have survived both surgeries yet even lucid I am nagged by the sense of nothingness in that black place. It's almost like sleeping without recalling that you dreamed but more sinister. When you sleep and dream, you are seemingly assured that you are going to wake up to recall the dream. But, when you are asleep or unconscious with no dream and only darkness, there is nothing to tether to for assurance. There is no foothold on reality.

It's not frightening to me but it does make me aware of a plane of consciousness that is not yet given a name. An unknown place. Maybe that is what they mean by 'the great beyond.'

Can you see a white light or a tunnel? I can honestly say that I've never seen anything but black space. I think if I did see something that suggested an afterlife or indicated a clear separation from the body, I would already be halfway to Heaven.

Existing in a virtual reality

Our technology-driven lives make it possible to remove ourselves from 'real life'. If we have the access and skills, we can step in and out of it at will.

Here I am at a café in Corpus Christi. There are at least 150 people in this place with me, yet I've only spoken to three. I only spoke to them because I wanted to make a purchase. Now that I have my meal, I have no need or interest in speaking to anyone else here. Why should I? I have the technology to shut them out.

I am wearing headphones, listening to music from my computer. I am listening to music that I like. I am not forced to listen to the easy-listening muzak that stores pump in to keep customers in a buying mood. I put my music into my computer and can retrieve and play it whenever I want. The music not only entertains me, it also keeps out the voices of others. So, even in a large group, I hear almost no one.

I am working on my laptop. I brought it with me so that I could sit at the bar and type. The elderly woman to the left of me, the one who had trouble getting up to the bar but is now comfortably seated and enjoying her pastry, is politely trying not to read as I type, but she is finding it difficult. Maybe she doesn't realize that I can see her in my peripheral vision. Maybe the fact that she isn't supposed to look compels her to do so.

I don't mind. I understand. I occasionally look to the right to see my other neighbor navigate her FaceBook account. She's listening to her iPod, so, like me, she is in her own space. We all share the same physical place (the bar) but we are not together there. Two of us have ascended to virtual planes.

In some ways, I am the master of my universe. In other ways, I have removed myself from society. Is there danger in that? I don't know. I don't think so. If I were sitting here without a laptop and headphones, would I be chatting with my neighbor? Would I be asking her about her dessert? No. I'd be staring off into space, enjoying my lunch and the internal dialogue that constantly runs through my brain. I wouldn't be any more engaged with the inhabitants of the coffee bar than I am at this very moment.

I think technology has changed us. We multitask more than ever. We control many input devices – for music, information, communication, entertainment and health -- designed to ensure that our personal preferences are attended to on demand. We rely more on the virtual world to fulfill our needs than we rely on physical strangers. The virtual world is not our escape; it is our primary living space.

And the elderly woman next to me, the one who doesn't seem to get the coffee bar culture, has eased down from her stool and left, untouched by the technology that envelopes me. If she hadn't jostled my chair, I may never have noticed her leave. Or care. I'm in my old little world here – my virtual reality.

Can you pass a citizenship test?

Are you a U.S. citizen? Have you been all of your life? What if you had to take a test to keep your citizenship? Are you up to the task? Try to answer the following questions.

The actual naturalization test is an oral exam, but I'll make it easy on you. Here is not only a written test, but a multiple choice one. Enjoy!

1. What is the supreme law of the land?
	A. The Bill of Rights
	B. The Declaration of Independence
	C. The Pickwick Papers
	D. The Constitution
2. What is one right or freedom from the First Amendment?
	A. petition the government
	B. public education
	C. Manifest Destiny
	D. to bear arms
3. Which one is a branch of the government?
	A. Federal
	B. Financial
	C. Legislative
	D. Primary
4. What stops one branch of government from becoming too powerful?
	A. Yin and Yang
	B. Checks and Balances
	C. Church and State
	D. Liberal and Conservative
5. If both the President and the Vice President can no longer serve, who becomes President?
	A. Secretary of State
	B. Secretary of the Senate
	C. Speaker of the House
	D. Chief Justice of the Supreme Court
6. What is the name of the Speaker of the House of Representatives now?
	A. Nancy Pelosi
	B. Newt Gingrich
	C. Dan Quayle

D. John G. Roberts Jr.

7. What is one promise you make when you become a United States citizen?

    A. To live in the United States
    B. To give up loyalty to other countries
    C. To vote
    D. To obey the Commander in Chief

8. Who lived in America before the Europeans arrived?

    A. the French
    B. Italians
    C. Spaniards
    D. Native Americans

9. Which of the following is one of the 13 original states?

    A. Vermont
    B. Connecticut
    C. Florida
    D. West Virginia

10. What is one thing Benjamin Franklin is not famous for?

    A. U.S. diplomat
    B. First Postmaster General of the United States
    C. President of Harvard University
    D. Started the first free libraries

Score:

8-10 correct -- Congratulations, you are a civic-minded citizen of the United States of America.

6-7 correct – Good job. You are proud to be an American and it shows.

4-5 correct – You should brush up on your U.S. History.

0-3 correct – INS called. They want to talk to you.

The answers to this quiz are: 1D,2D,3C,4B,5B,6A,7B,8D,9B,10C

Adrian Jackson is a freelance writer in Beeville, Texas. She was born a citizen of the United States of America, though she hasn't lived here all of her life. For more fun questions on citizenship, go to http://www.uscis.gov/files/nativedocuments/100q.pdf.

So you want to be a U.S. citizen?

Some of you asked if it was the same article that ran in a national newspaper. No it was not. I used the questions and correct answers on the citizenship website and made up the multiple choices on my own. I never read that article, though we used the same source.

I got an incredible response from the last citizenship article. Here are some more questions for you to mull over:

1. In what month is the new President inaugurated?
   - A. January
   - B. May
   - C. July
   - D. November
2. How many times may a Senator or Congressman be re-elected?
   - A. Twice.
   - B. There is no limit.
   - C. Until he/she is 67 years-old.
   - D. Six times.
3. In what year was the Constitution written?
   - A. The Constitution was written in 1787.
   - B. The Constitution was written in 1776.
   - C. The Constitution was written in1812.
   - D. The Constitution was written in 1492.
4. What is the name of the ship that brought the Pilgrims to America?
   - A. The Pinta
   - B. The Titanic
   - C. The Mayflower
   - D. The Spanish Armada
5. Who wrote The Star-Spangled Banner?
   - A. Francis Scott Key
   - B. Thomas Jefferson
   - C. Benjamin Franklin
   - D. Thomas Edison
6. For how long do we elect each member of the House of Representatives?
   - A. For six years
   - B. For four years
   - C. For two years
   - D. For life

7. What makes up Congress?
    A. The Senate
    B. The House of Representatives
    C. The President and his Cabinet
    D. The Senate and the House of Representatives
8. Independence Day celebrates independence from whom?
    A. Independence from France
    B. Independence from Native Americans
    C. Independence from Great Britain
    D. Independence from Plymouth Rock
9. How many stars are there on our flag?
    A. There are 50 stars on our flag.
    B. There are 13 stars on our flag.
    C. There are 100 stars on our flag.
    D. There are 48 stars on our flag.
10. How many voting members are in the House of Representatives?
    A. 100
    B. 435
    C. 50
    D. 215

Answers: 1A,2B,3A,4C,5A,6C,7D,8C,9A,10B

Is that moron your cousin?

A recent scientific journal article concludes that we carry one to four percent of the Neanderthal genome. This suggests that at some point, Neanderthals dipped into our gene pool.

Picture it... tens of thousands of years ago ... a handful of hot *homo sapien* chicas sitting around a puddle of primordial goo, shooting the breeze when along comes a bunch of *homo neanderthalensis* with game. Eyes were batted. Flirting was done. One thing led to another and ... bam... interbreeding. Fast forward to the future and we've got the DNA of the species we've long outlasted and, frankly, looked down upon.

Neanderthals earned their name from the site where the first skeleton was found in a cave in Germany. 'Thal' is German for valley, so the first remnant of the species was found in the Neander Valley near Dusseldorf.

The word Neanderthal has come to mean course, ill-mannered and uncouth. When we call someone a Neanderthal, we really mean 'big, dumb, jerk,' don't we? We have long believed that our species is superior to the Neanderthal and other sub-humans but in reality our ancestors must have found some positive qualities in them.

They were not all brawn and boorishness. They had some skills. They wore rudimentary clothing and lived in shelters. They knew how to build fires. They could hunt. They used and designed tools to fill various needs. Scientists believe that Neanderthal buried their dead and marked the graves of loved ones with ornamentation.

Some of our ancestors must have found the Neanderthal attractive. Maybe it was the sloped foreheads or bushy eyebrows. Maybe it was the red hair. Maybe it was the way they spoke in poetic grunts and groans.

I'm sure that *homo sapien* dads tried to stop this dating and mating. They must have suffered to watch their daughters fawn over these clods. They must have said to their daughters, 'Don't go out with that moron. He's a Neanderthal!'

Poor Nean. He must have had a heck of a time wooing that smart and sophisticated girl who was clearly way, way out of his league. He must have thought that she was a little stuck-up with all of that walking upright nonsense. He must have found her rounded forehead and large brain exotic.

Over the course of our human history, Neanderthals have been treated with a heavy dose of disrespect. We looked down on them as knuckle-dragging mouth-breathers. Maybe they were actually very nice sub-humans. Some of our great-great-great-great-great … great-great-grandparents certainly thought so.

In the end, I guess, Neanderthals won out. They didn't disappear from the Earth as we previously thought. They went into hiding. They hibernated. They slipped into the abyss, dormant, waiting to be rediscovered. They've been on the journey with us the whole time. Fascinating, isn't it?

Maybe Neanderthals deserve better than we've given them for eons. After all, they are our cousins.

Doogie Houser, M.D.

During a recent visit to the emergency room, when the doctor left the room I leaned over to my friend and asked, 'What is he, like, twelve?' I've reached that point in my life where some people in positions of authority are younger than me. This doctor (or maybe he was a resident) wasn't ten years younger than me but he might have been quite close to that.

I've gotten to that stage in my life where my doctors, lawyers, professors and insurance agents are my age and sometimes younger. This is unsettling. I imagine he grew up on Transformer cartoons and hums U2 songs while waiting for my scans to come back. I imagine that he got drunk on Zima in college and that he thinks that Chris Rock is the freaking awesomest comedian, like, ever. None of these visuals are comforting when I am waiting for this pre-teen to make an emergency diagnosis.

The ER didn't have much of a bedside manner. That got me to thinking that they just don't emphasize the importance of interacting with patients in today's medical schools. Doctors don't seem to learn to be empathetic or interactive or any of those things patients crave when we are sick.

I want a doctor who will use my name, even if he has to read if off of my chart. I want a doctor who looks me in the eye and talks to me, not *at* me. I want someone who can take notes while talking to me. I was a reporter for many years so I know this is not impossible or unreasonable.

I want a doctor who will make me feel welcomed in his office. He may be there every day, but I am not. As a matter of fact, the only time I visit him is when I am really sick. I want to be made to feel like a guest.

I want him to listen. No, really listen.

I want someone who will let me ramble a little. Sometimes when I ramble, I am processing. I discover new bits of information in this processing mode, so it is a critical part of my thought process.

I want him to trust me. I may not have a medical degree, but I know my own body better than anyone else. I should be able to work with my doctor on a diagnosis and treatment plan. I may not know all of those fancy Latin words but when it come to me or my family, I am a great diagnostician. I know what is not normal and I am not an idiot, so I'd like to be given credence and respect for my opinions and preferences.

Growing up, I saw the same doctor for more than 10 years. My doctor was in a practice with his brother, dad and mother. One or another was also the primary caregiver for my sisters, aunt, grandfather and several other family members, so they knew a lot about our family history. This made it easy to be a patient, because I had a personal relationship with my doctor. A history. I felt comfortable and well cared for by him.

My childhood doctor showed me a high level of personal care that I've come to expect from all doctors. Sometimes I get it but most of the time I don't.

Dr. Doogie didn't have it, though in his defense, he is young and may mask his lack of experience and confidence behind an uber-professional persona. Hopefully, his bedside manner will get better with time.

The end is nigh

Note to reader: I am sorry to inform you that you are going to die. We all are. I cannot tell you when, where or how, but I can unequivocally promise you that one-by-one we are all going to die.

When I was a teenager, there was a looming threat that African Killer Bees would swoop in and sting us all to death. While Africanized Bees are a serious threat and hundreds have died in this country from attacks, they have yet to take over the world. But when you are young and dumb you immediately adopt a sense of dread and doom.

This week, we are faced with the menace of a Swine Flu that is unfolding in our very backyards. While we were able to largely ignore the Avian flu that spread through Asia, we cannot ignore the Mexican outbreak that has slipped over our borders (with no passport) and taken hold in greater San Antonio. Schools and governments have closed and the Center for Disease Control and Prevention is on the case.

In an effort to inform my daughter about taking extra precautions at school to limit exposure, I managed to scare the bejesus out of her. The end result was that she crawled into my bed in the middle of the night after a nightmare (probably about rampant, sneezing pigs).

We'll all do what we can to protect our families and this influenza will eventually pass, only to be replaced by the next civilization-ending scare.

If you watch the news, read the paper, surf the Net or listen to your local psychic, you will be frequently warned that the end of the world is nigh. They are all correct. We've occupied this planet for thousands or billions of years (depending on who your source is) and every day takes us closer to the last one for each of us and for all of us.

My daughter asked me if the world was coming to an end in 2012 and I asked, 'What the hell are they teaching you up at that school?!' More likely, she gets this perception from television, books and the movies. The History Channel and Nat Geo put out almost daily warnings steeped in innuendo and slathered with scientific and theological supposition. Films like *Knowing* and *I Am Legend,* and books like *Left Behind* keep the concept of End Times in the forefront of our consciousness. Is the increase of End-of-Days movies a harbinger of the coming of the end or is the threat of the end of the world a cash cow for book and movie writers? Hmmmm.

This is not the first time the end has been predicted by prophets, clairvoyants, oracles, diviners, soothsayers, prognosticators, seers, sages and sign carriers. It's good business because eventually they will all be proven right. The world will come to an end.

At the end, many of us will die but we were going to die anyway and its entirely possible that most of us won't realize that we have approached that moment of death until a millisecond before it overtakes us. When the end comes will those who forewarned us, take the time to say 'I told ya so'? Will it matter at that point?

There will be signs that the world is coming to an end. Some believe the signs are already playing themselves out. Certainly a giant meteor hurling toward the Earth faster than the speed of light would be a good indication of the end. Four horsemen descending from the heavens would be a clue. A nuclear blast would be a tip-off. But, does that mean that we have to treat every crisis as the last? I don't think so. When the world ends I hope I've done the right things to prepare, but, for today, I'll just pray with fervor and hope for the best.

10 things to do before I die

The new thing is to make a list of things you want to do before you die. Some common items to make the list are backpacking in Europe (done it), earning a degree (done it), sky diving (never gonna happen), weight loss (grrrrr), learning a language (done it), meeting a celebrity (done it), traveling (done it), running with the bulls (are you nucking futs?!), swimming with dolphins and winning the lottery (cash payout=$3).

I don't make lists. I don't even make New Year's resolutions. But in the spirit of adventure, I'm going to give this a whorl:

1. **Visit Australia.** A friend of mine lives there, so this would be the perfect time to go and avoid hotel costs but the flight is expensive.

2. **Spend the day in McColl, South Carolina.** My great-grandmother was born and raised there. My oral family history is there and I want to dig into the archives at the library and courthouse to see how far back my McLucas and Demery families go.

3. **Record my grandmother's memories.** I talk to my grandmother all the time but I don't really *talk* to her. I wonder what kind of priceless stories she has to tell.

4. **Take my daughter skiing.** I've skied in Austria, Switzerland and Germany, but my daughter hasn't. I don't really enjoy skiing but she should experience it at least once.

5. **Publish a novel.** I've completed two novels and started a million others but I've never taken the time to have them published.

6. **Pay someone to clean my house.** I don't do a good job at house cleaning. If I had time, I'd do better. I've been trying to find money in my budget to hire someone but it hasn't happened yet.

7. **Adopt a child.** I can't have more children but there is room in my life for one more. I've set goals for this but it will be years before I achieve it.

8. **Earn a Ph.D.** I am actively working on this. It's going to take about six more years but I'm committed to it.

9. **Go on vacation with my sisters and their families.** The last time we all got together was in 1992 when only two of us were married and one of us had kids. My oldest sister, already a grandmother, has three adult children, so it is becoming harder to pull this together.

10. **Live in Europe again.** I lived in Germany for 11 years. My memories are idyllic and I want to go back to that experience.

Dying with Dignity

I'm going to die.

This shouldn't come as a surprise to anyone. We are all going to die. You are going to die, too.

We don't think about death nearly as much as we should. We don't have to be morose about it. We can be practical. We actually should be practical. When I attempted to speak to my mother-in-law about custody of my daughter in the event of my death, she started to cry. When I mailed a copy of my will to my mother and sisters, they thought I was nuts. But these are things we have to be open and honest about.

I don't want to be hooked up to life support. I don't really understand how medically your brain can function when your heart doesn't or vice versa but I want no part of that business. I want to make a clean break. My mother thinks I want to donate my body to science. She actually tells people this. I've heard her. No matter what I say, this scenario lives on in her head. I have to warn my sisters not to let her within 50 feet of my dead body until my true wishes are met. I have nothing against people who make this decision but the idea of medical students giggling at the stretch marks around my mid-section is more than I can bear, even in death.

I want to donate my organs. All of 'em. I want to have a great big organ giveaway. Get 'em while they're hot. Bring your own cooler. I base my decision on the belief in a benevolent God who will kindly replace whatever I need when I get where I'm going. I don't think this subject is covered in the Bible. Can someone look into that and get back to me?

Since there won't be much of me left after they've plucked my body clean, I'd like to be cremated. I think cremation is a very efficient means of disposal. I don't really care where my ashes go. At that point they are no longer useful to me. But if they were scattered around the base of a tree maybe that would do the tree some good. My decision leaves me with no grave marker. That means there will be no tangible evidence of my death. So, how will I leave my mark? I think what you do on Earth is a better testament of life than a beautifully etched stone. Here is what I'm leaving behind:

- **Descendants.** The birth of a child who grows up to have another child and so on is a continuation of the lives of all those who contributed to it. I leave behind my genetic

code and the morals and values I've passed on to my daughter.
- **Community service.** I've impacted the lives of hundreds of girls through Girl Scouts. That's important to me. I leave behind volunteer work on committees that seek to improve our community.
- **Written works.** My articles will appear 50 years from now in scrapbooks. They will be referenced in book reports. They will be used as source material for future articles. Every photo and article is a record of someone's life or a defining moment in local history. Long after I'm forgotten my work lives on.
- **Legacy.** I think this is the culmination of who you are. I'm still trying to figure that out. I'll have to get back to you.

I know that when I'm dead I won't actually care about these details but, right now, I am the steward of me. I want to know that what I leave on this Earth, whether it's a lung or a letter it will make a difference to someone even in a small way.

To be blessed enough to have all your directives in death is to die with dignity.

What I want in a president

I want a president who is at least as smart as me. I don't think anyone would have to work too hard to eclipse me. Mensa ain't knocking down my door, if you know what I mean. I think it is appropriate to expect the U.S. President to be an intellectual and to be recognized as one of the greater (as opposed to the lesser) minds in our country.

I want a president who is respectful of world leaders. Chavez and Ahmadinejad are world leaders that Americans generally abhor, but they are, in fact, leaders in their respective countries. There should be a basic level of gentlemanliness and good manners extended to them by our president and his representatives based on that.

I want a president who is a proven problem solver. I don't think there is a corporation or university in this country that would consider hiring an untested leader. I think we should have the same standards in the highest office.

I want a president who has a broad knowledge of the world – geographically and politically. I want a president who is an expert in at least on region of the world, beyond North America. I want someone who has an understanding of global structure and how each country's actions influence all other countries and doesn't look at the U.S. with an isolationist or hegemonic perspective.

I want a fiscally conservative president. I want someone who looks at the bottom line and future economic impact before approving a budget. I want someone who safeguards our children's future even if being tough hurts feelings. I want a president who preaches fiscal responsibility to all government intuitions and practices what he preaches through word and deed. I want a president who can make tough calls and is the last line of defense against the pork that is siphoning off this country's resources.

I want a socially responsible president. I want a president who supports a strong work ethic, but is committed to helping those who need it most. I want a president who will get the nation's socially-dependent off the dole by occasionally pulling the rug out from under them and shaking up their complacency. I want a president who will put more resources behind programs for kids – health, education, well-being and protection.

I want a president who is committed to education. I want someone who will recognize the individuality of children and students and commit to developing educational opportunities that appeal to each one, not all of them at once. I want someone who will listen to teachers and move towards giving them what they need to educate our children and not hide behind unions, movements and catchy phrases.

I want a president who is able to work with anyone and everyone for the betterment of the people of the United States, without consideration of political affiliation.

I want a president who will talk to me. Really talk. I want to listen to someone who tells the truth, speaks honestly and frankly, and doesn't try to shield me from bad news or bad decisions. I want a president whose speeches aren't vetted by those who measure words for their political capital. I want eloquent speeches with real meaning that demonstrate the power of the president and the might of this nation. I want to be able to say, 'I didn't agree with a word the president said, but that was a fine speech.'

Name-calling hurts

A presidential hopeful was recently asked, 'How do we beat the bitch?' If you've not heard about this, 'the bitch' is Hillary Clinton.

First, let me apologize to readers for my vulgarity. I assure you that there is both a purpose and a point. Please read on.

Secondly, I am no fan of Hillary Clinton. I will not vote for her. This article is not political nor an indication of support.

The speaker in this case was a woman. I am especially disheartened by that because *we* should know better. Women have worked long and hard to break through stereotypes that hold us back from achieving our dreams. When things like this happen, we women collectively slide backward towards becoming second-class citizens, bitches and whores.

There is never a good reason to call someone by anything other than their given name. To do so is bad manners, poor breeding and disrespectful. It is rude and, in many instances, offensive.

If Clinton were a man, would she be referred to as a bitch? She is not the first successful woman to be called out like that. What does this say about the equality of women in this country? If Clinton were a man, would anyone even consider attaching a moniker to her name? There isn't even a male equivalent word for bitch in our vocabulary.

Why did the woman feel comfortable making such an offensive statement? She probably said it for shock value. She must have been pretty assured that there would be no immediate backlash. But, even if she was in a room full of staunch Clinton haters, why was she certain that she wouldn't be reprimanded? What does it say about those in the room, who were neither shocked nor openly offended by the woman's question? Some snickered at the remark. The presidential candidate sidestepped it. Even when he was later criticized for not addressing it, he did not make a moral statement about the inappropriateness of the word.

Is it so common that we can toss it around at will? Is it such an acceptable word that it can be used in open forum? I can't help but question if it had been, 'How do we beat the nigger?' Would the same group have laughed? I doubt it. So, why is one offensive name more acceptable than another? Why is one word less shocking or volatile than another? Both are meant to hurt. Spic, fag, freak. We know which words do damage and we know how to use them.

And what about respect for the highest office in our land? Doesn't running for president afford you a minimal level of respect? It used to. What if Clinton becomes our next president? Would you want to be the one who called her a bitch? If someone is willing to go public with such a vulgar remark, how will that person refer to her if she becomes president?

I'm not saying that using the word is wrong. You can use whatever words you'd like. Sticks and stones and all that. I know you hear the word everywhere. They use it on Friends. I hear it used as an adjective to describe certain types of behavior. Beeach is a ghetto derivative that has become a mainstream word that kids like to use. But, as a society, we have to raise the level of discourse. We have other words. We are not base, ignorant animals. We are not beneath civility or decency. We don't have to devalue ourselves by using bar room words that incite riots and pierce daggers into the hearts of those they hit hardest.

Hillary Clinton deserves better than that. We all do.

We can all get along

In this hotly contested presidential race, I'm glad that I can still talk to my friends. Republican, Democrat, red, blue, Liberal, Conservative, Moderate and all points in between don't come between us.

One of my friends is running for reelection. I've voted for her in the past and if I still lived in her district, I'd vote for her again. She is good at what she does. She is a wife, mother and role model. She is ultra-Conservative and I don't agree with her position on the theory of evolution, but that has never been an obstacle to friendship.

Another buddy has never voted in his life. He registered to vote when he registered for Selective Service as he was required to do by law at the age of 18. He is now in his 40s and has never, ever participated in a single election on any level. I get a little angry when he rails about politics because I believe that if you don't take part in the process, you can't dispute the outcome. But we've been friends for 20 years and engage in some very interesting and intense political discussions.

One friend shares my views on many issues. We are both pretty conservative, but sit on opposite sides of the political fence. Sometimes it is hard for me to understand how we can agree so much. One of us is clearly in the wrong party. Though we think in tandem on many topics, there are a couple of issues for which we are diametrically opposed. But I don't begrudge her her opinion. I love my friend and though we can talk on a broad range of topics, there are certain political doors that have to remain closed to preserve our friendship.

Another friend is of the old-school Democratic Party Liberals. Her politics are of the LBJ era. She is socially conscience and her point of view on most issues comes with a protectionist's umbrella over those in society who need the government most.

One of my friends is a Tri-State Area Liberal. She grew up in New Jersey, where she still lives. She used to participate in protests when she was younger and was even hauled off to jail once for it. She likes to call herself a radical. We never discuss politics beyond perfunctory comments because I agree with almost none of her politics.

And then there is me. I'm a Democrat. I couldn't imagine being otherwise. I'm not an exceptionally loyal one, but I registered in 1988 as a Democrat and have been since. My first presidential election was between George H.W. Bush and Michael Dukakis and I was very proud to be able to take part.

It is my belief that those who take the most virulent positions on issues have the least amount of knowledge about them. Every issue has two sides and our ability to meet on common ground and work through our differences is what has sustained our democracy. If you listen to politicians you may get the impressions that we all fall on the farthest fringes of one side or the other, but my experience has been that we exist more in the middle than anywhere else. Do you find that to be true?

Go vote

I voted last week, so I am done with the election process. At this point, nothing can happen that will change the vote that I've already cast. For me, the remaining election coverage is for entertainment purposes only. So this is my last column about politics, but we had fun, didn't we?

I like to vote early. I voted on Election Day for the first and last time in 1988. Since then, I've voted absentee or early. Some people enjoy casting a vote on the national voting day, but I don't care to. I'm more of the vote-now-in-case-you-forget variety. I wanted to vote last Monday but couldn't get away from work. I wanted to vote last Tuesday but had to run a different errand instead. So, I voted last Wednesday. If I were faced with the same obstacles on Nov. 4, maybe I would miss my opportunity to vote. The scenario concerns me so I vote early.

It doesn't really matter when you vote as long as you take part in the process.

Our ancestors protested, marched, were beaten and died so that we could all have the right to vote. The political movements of women, African-Americans, servicemembers and Hispanic-Americans have resulted in the expansion of the right to vote in the United States. This is a precious gift that billions of adults on this planet are denied for a lifetime.

If you don't vote and forfeit your responsibility to the government of our country, you don't get to complain for the next four years. If you abdicate your role in the democracy, you lose your voice in it. So go vote!

If you've doggedly followed the issues from the beginning and this is the natural conclusion of a very long race, go vote.

If you think that your vote doesn't really count and one candidate is worse than the other, go vote.

If you plan to write in Ron Paul, Ralph Nader or Mickey Mouse, go vote.

If your choice is the most handsome, has the prettiest wife or wears the snazziest suits, go vote.

If you just became eligible to vote and this is your first presidential election, go vote.

If you think that one candidate is the Antichrist and only a vote for the other can save us all from annihilation, go vote.

If you are so loyal to your party that you vote a straight party ticket, go vote (but make sure that you talk to an election clerk before doing this so that you understand how to do it correctly and don't accidentally disqualify your own vote).

If you've taken three tests to see which of your views are in line with the candidates and based your decisions on that, go vote.

If the words 'change' or 'maverick' stir something in your soul, go vote.

If you could care less about local politics but want to participate on a national scale, go vote.

If you've never voted once in your life, go vote.

If you've voted in every election since you were 18 and you were planning to go anyway, go vote.

If you find this ridiculous list of imaginary voters annoying and condescending, go vote.

Your vote counts.

On a more personal note, I was very much a fan of Tim Russert. So much so, that I couldn't write a column about him when he died though I wanted to. Russert's participation in Election Night coverage will be missed. Thank God for the time that he spent on this earth and for the impact that he had on the lives of many.

Change is coming; We are moving on up

We finally did it, America. We wrangled power out of the hands of the status quo and took it for ourselves. This is the dawn of a new era.

Barrack Obama is the first post-Baby Boomer president in what has turned out to be a short run for such a large demographic. Baby Boomers are Americans born after WWII between 1945 and 1952. Some extend the generation into the 1960s, but I think Obama is clearly *not* a Baby Boomer.

Bill Clinton, born in 1946, was the first U.S. President too young to have served in World War II. He was a Baby Boomer. George W. Bush, also born in 1946, was the second Baby Boomer in the White House. He is the son of a WWII veteran. President George H.W. Bush, along with Dwight D. Eisenhower, John F. Kennedy, Lyndon B. Johnson, Richard M. Nixon, Gerald R. Ford and Ronald Reagan, served in the Second World War. President Jimmy Carter was a student at the U.S. Naval Academy during the war.

Baby Boomers may make a comeback in subsequent elections, but in four years more Gen X'ers and Gen Y'ers will reach political maturity and possibly push the Boomers out of the competitive arena.

So, Gen X has moved into the White House and we've brought little kids, reality TV and rap music with us.

We Gen X'ers are maligned for our self-centeredness, bluntness and cynicism, but like the generation before us, our experiences have shaped who we are. We grew up with cable television and house keys on strings around our necks. We grew up terrified of catching AIDS, but fearless in our relentless pursuit of financial success. We grew up in the shadow of the Atlanta Child Murders and under the influence of Public Enemy. We saw the fall of the Berlin Wall and the rise of the Nikkei. We saw Germany reunified and Yugoslavia torn apart. We live in dual-income families and buy everything with credit cards. We fought Iraq in Operation Desert Storm and when that wasn't enough, many of us went back to fight them again.

As we move into positions previously held by Boomers, we take on a great sense of responsibility. We know what has to be done. We are ready. We don't have to be lectured about what we don't know and how it used to be. We get it. You Boomers have raised us right. Now it's time to see what we can do.

We have great expectations for this country. This year, our mantra is 'hope and change.' Barrack Obama, for better or worse, is our leader. Gen X is moving on up and there ain't no stopping us now. Gen X rules.

And remember... be nice to us. We're in charge now.

Adrian Jackson is a freelance writer in Beeville, Texas. Born in 1970, she is solidly Gen X.

Great-grandmother leaves a lasting legacy

I hung a photo of my great-grandmother above a picture of me, pregnant, on my wall. The combination of the photos represents over a century of my family tree. My great-grandmother's facsimile presence in my living room brings me unending comfort and strength.

Maggie McLucas Way was my great-grandmother. She was born Sept. 1, 1896 in McColl, South Carolina. She ultimately moved to Chicago, then Newark, New Jersey, where her kids were raised. She died months shy of her 102nd birthday.

Because I was blessed with too many grandmothers, I called her Grandma Way, not to be confused with Grandma Jackson, Granny, Oma Elwine, or Grandma.

When I look at the photo of Grandma Way, I can see the face of my grandmother, my mother, my aunt Karen and myself. I see my mother's fingers as clearly as if they were attached to her hands, not her grandmother's. I see my Aunt Gloria's hair, fine as silk. I see my grandmother's nose.

Maggie was a beautiful woman. In the photo, her eyebrows are severely arched in a way that tells me that keeping them in order was very important to her at the time. She was short and hearty. There is no trace of willow or frailty to her. The dress she's wearing was fashionable but not new. I don't' know when the photo was taken, but Maggie looks to be in her late 20s or early 30s.

She was a laundress by profession. That may be why the fabric on her sleeves has an upward curl to it – the constant position of her arms. She worked for a Catholic church.

I did not know her as she was in the photo. My earliest recollection is of her and my great-grandfather living in a retirement community. I remember her as the lady with the cookies. She always had Lorna Doones for us to eat, though we were admonished if we were greedy and ate all of Grandaddy's snacks. She would part her hair down the middle and let her great-grand-daughters take turns brushing and braiding it for hours. She crocheted things like doilies, pillows and a Southern belle toilet paper cover. She was a longtime member of Israel Memorial AME Church in Newark, New Jersey. Her name and her husband's, Olden C. Way, can be found on a plaque because of their decades of service and support to the church that several family members still attend.

The last time I saw Maggie was a few days after her 100th birthday bash. She was living with one of my grandmother's sisters by then, needing constant care. She called me by my sister's name but I was pleased that she was lucid. I knew by her age and her rheumy eyes that I was saying goodbye to her.

She lived for almost two more years. My daughter was born before she died, but the two of them never met. Maggie died just months before I was able to bring my daughter home for a visit.

Her photo reminds me that continuity and unity hold the many generations – living and deceased -- of my family together. Her presence reminds me of the important stories about that I can pass down to my own daughter. She is a reminder of how one small woman can leave such a lasting legacy.

Adrian Jackson is a freelance writer in Beeville, Texas. She is a descendant of Albert McLucas and Rebecca Dimery, Maggie's parents, who were both born in 1871.

Census reveals forgotten details about family tree

My daughter and I have t-shirts from a recent family reunion. Albert McLucas-Rebecca Dimery: 1871 is printed on the front under a large tree. Albert and Rebecca are my great-grandmother Maggie McLucas Way's parents.

When my daughter asked me what 1871 meant, I took advantage of a teaching moment and decided to take her on a tour of our family tree. Both Albert and Rebecca were born in 1871 in South Carolina. They were married in 1889. Albert was a farmer who owned his own land and Rebecca was a housewife. We pulled up the 1900 census and saw my great-great-grandparent's names, the names of their children (Maggie was three years old) and the names of Rebecca's parents, who lived with them.

This is one of the remarkable benefits of the Census. Each one is a wealth of knowledge. Each is like an administrative archeological dig. As long as you have the names, you can find almost anyone. The U.S. Census Bureau records are available from as far back as 1790 in some cases. There are also birth, death and marriage records. Most importantly, all of this information is available on Ancestry.com through our local library.

So, we were sitting in the Joe Barnhart Bee County Library browsing through census records and decided to see if we could pull up the census data from Rebecca's parents. We opened 1880 census records and found Niell and Lota E. Dimery. Niell was listed as a farmer in the 1880 census. He was a native South Carolinian, born in February 1850, and was classified as mulatto – a man of mixed race. His wife, Lota, was born in South Carolina in March 1853. She was white. She was listed as a housewife. They had three children in 1880 (Rebecca was nine) and an unrelated 10-year-old boy living in their home.

Wait? What? White? Huh? Lota Dimery was a white woman?! When I saw the "W" under race, I did a double take. Lota Dimery was a white woman married to a mulatto man in post-Civil War South Carolina?!

My first thought was to dismiss it as a mistake. But then I thought, *who the hell makes that kind of mistake in 1880?* I sat there flummoxed. How did this white woman get into my family tree? Where did she come from? How did she marry a man of color in 1880?

I dug and dug and found something interesting but never fully answered the question of Lota Dimery. Here's what I found:

John Dimery was a free man of color. What his actual race was is unrecorded. On the 1820 census, Dimery was listed as "mulatto," a word that was used for Native Americans, free people of color and those of ambiguous origins.

According to another website, John founded a community in rural South Carolina that was made up of members of the Waccamaw and Lumbee Tribes, former slaves, those of Spanish and Portuguese descent and later Civil War deserters. He owned 600 acres of the settlement and was a driving force in education, commerce and politics in the county. He was a registered Democrat.

The people of the Dimery Settlement intermarried with little regard to race. Whites in the surrounding areas were suspicious of questionable marriages but nothing much was done about it. A 1921 court case was filed on grounds of miscegenation against two white men who married Dimery women but I wasn't able to find what the outcome was.

I can't definitively say that I am related to John Dimery but I'm looking into it. I think Dimery might be a family name, not a slave name as I'd assumed all these years.

How Neill Dimery came to be married to Lota? I cannot say with certainty. That's a story for another day.

Adrian Jackson is a freelance writer in Beeville, Texas. She mailed in her census form a week ago.

Reality TV does nothing for me

My philosophy on reality television is that if I wanted reality I would turn the boob tube off and get a life. But there are times in the day when I don't want reality; I want a fantasy. So, I turn on the television.

I don't want to watch people try to save their marriage. I don't care who the baby's daddy is. I don't want to see people pretend to be entertainers. Dr. Phil doesn't say anything I want to hear.

I like television shows with actors. I want to watch doctors performing surgeries underwater using ink pens. I want to see a kid who is a geeky high-schooler by day and a pop star by night. I want to see siblings that live together in a home with their biological mother and father and no matter what kind of trouble they find themselves in, it will all be resolved within 30 minutes.

I don't watch that much television. I watch about two hours a day during the week. That includes the morning news, the show that lulls me to sleep and the 30 minutes of prime time I squeeze in. I'm too busy with my real life to find time for the escape I crave.

But I do watch TV. I'm not ashamed to say that I enjoy watching television. It drives me crazy when people say they don't. Whenever people say that, there is always haughtiness in their voice isn't there? *Oh, we don't watch TV. We prefer to act out scenes from Hamlet and read Russian poetry.*

How can you not watch TV? How can you not own a TV? Don't you at least want to see the news or keep up with hurricane warnings? Don't you just crave mindless, deadpan entertainment? You can't read all the time.

I like game shows. I like morning news. I like documentaries. There is a handful of reality-documentaries that I enjoy, but by and large, I don't watch reality TV. I watch some medical shows. I like that one about the weight loss doctors – father and son-- who help people who are over 300 pounds. I find it both fascinating and heart wrenching to see lives changed by surgical intervention. I like shows that keep up with medical miracle kids. Some of the stories are difficult to watch, but all are captivating. I watched a show about a little boy who Chinese doctors were able to save despite all odds. When he finally went home, he caught an infection and died. I cried for hours.

I like shows that are educational. When I was a kid our television got stuck on PBS. My mother was overjoyed. She kept that TV for years. We learned a lot.

I like Discovery Channel, the History Channel and National Geographic. I don't like that they renamed themselves Nat Geo. Television stations shouldn't have nicknames. *My name is National Geographic but you can call me Nat Geo.* Who are they trying to market that channel to with that unhip truncation of a name?

I like travel shows. I've never taken a cruise so it's fun to watch and dream. I've travelled to many old European cities so it's fun to watch and compare. Since I can't travel as much as I'd like, I get a lot of pleasure from teletravel.

But none of these kinds of shows are reality TV in my opinion. The term 'reality TV' has taken on a negative connotation over the years. Today, it means a contrived show that comes out of forcing strangers to live, date, lose weight or perform together. The show is actually a caricature of reality since all you see are the hissy-fits and offensive acts. There is no enjoyment in watching people misbehave. I can do without all of that drama. I don't want that in my real life or my fantasy.

I stumbled upon a show once where the boyfriend went out on a date while the girlfriend stayed home with his parents, who observed the date on the television. The parents and the girlfriend shared a running commentary on the date. I guess that is the draw.

The girl was exceptionally rude to the parents. Instead of calling her out on her behavior, the parents were equally rude to her. Only, none of them spoke to each other in normal voices. It was like they got together before the show and agreed to belittle each other. Okay, I'm going to say this and then you say that... It was like watching a poorly acted soap opera.

While on the subject, I don't watch soap operas either. I did have a brief stint when I was a teenager and those soap lives seemed so glamorous and fascinating. Now I see that they are just overly dramatic. Besides, they've added violence and witchcraft now. One show centered around a coven of witches. Give me a break!

Congratulations, graduates .... what's next for you?

Welcome to the next phase of your life. Let me warn you – no one's handing out gold stars up here. But you are an adult now. You don't really need one, right?

Have you made a responsible decision about your future? Are you going to college? College seems a lot like school but it is so different. First of all, you are making an investment in yourself. College pays off. Don't let anyone tell you otherwise. Secondly, college is your time to party. Don't worry, your parents don't mind that you'll stay out too late or join a fraternity. It's expected (as long as you don't forget the *real* reason you are there). Thirdly, unless you want to still work for minimum wage when you are in your 30s (this happens a lot sooner than you can imagine), you can't afford not to learn a trade or gain an education.

Are you firm in your decision not to go to college? That's okay. Get used to saying, 'Would you like fries with that shake?' There will always be a wealth of jobs out there for you. You will work the worst shifts for the lowest pay. You might have to work two jobs. You won't have health insurance so you'd better not get sick -- ever. You'll buy used cars for the rest of your life and you can forget about owning your own home – the bank doesn't lend to poor people. Oh yeah, and children of parents who don't value education grow up to not value it either. So your kids are going to be a problem.

Maybe you'll realize that you made a mistake and go to college later in life. That's a good choice but it won't be easy. You'll juggle a full-time job, a family and bills with earning Bs and Cs because you just don't have the time to study. You'll sit next to 18-year-olds who spend a great part of their days either partying or sleeping, yet can put up As on every test even though in your opinion they are all idiots. Be nice to them -- one of 'em is probably going to be your future boss or congressman.

If you want to be a regular person, you've got to go to college. If you want to be successful, you've got to work your tail off for the next ten years. Maybe you'll have reached the level of success you wanted or maybe the bar will have been raised higher by the time you get there. That's a risk. Success is all about risk.

You've got to decide now how far you are willing to go for success. You've got to figure out what you are willing to sacrifice to get what you want out of life. You might have to give up family, friends, a conscience, your soul. You might have to move to another city, another state, another country. This is a good time to decide where your allegiances and ethics lie. They will be questioned and you won't have time to prepare for the answer. You're going to have to rely on somebody at some point so you may as well start building bridges now. You'll thank your lucky stars that you have friends and colleagues that you can call on when your professional life gets out of whack and believe me, it might just follow a completely unexpected path.

Remember when you were a kid and you got five to ten awards each school year? Guess what? There are no awards given for good attendance. Not everyone is a winner and the playing field is never leveled. You are not on the playground anymore. People up here will claw and kick at you on their way up and grab hold of your collar as they are tumbling down. Some of the people you think are your friends are just using you to further their own agendas. Adults lie, cheat and steal. Sometimes bad things happen to you despite your greatest efforts to do good.

Being an adult is a lot harder than your parents make it seem. Welcome to the rest of your life.

20 years out of high school

I graduated from Vailsburg High School in 1988. Oh, my God! I've been out of high school for 20 years.

When I was in high school (back in the previous millennium) I had great friends and a bright future. I wanted to be a journalist and live somewhere other than home. Thumbs up on both accounts.

Back in high school, I hung out with a group of kids whose last names were Jackson. One of them was my sister but the others were of no relation. We were a little dorky. We were all high achievers and graduated at the tops of our classes. Most of the Jackson kids graduated before me so that by the time I was a senior, the group had pretty much disbanded. I have had no contact with a single one of them since I left school.

This was partially my fault, since no one went to the college I went to and after a year I moved to Europe. I stayed for 11 years and on the few occasions I went home there were only a handful of old friends that I made a point to contact.

My best friend was Maurcia. We joined colorguards together. We were both tall and awkward and didn't really fit in. The colorguards were a close-knit, snotty group of girls who liked to play nasty jokes. The only people I liked on the squad were my sister, her best friend and Maurcia, who became my best friend. We made it through try-outs together, even though I had to work the hardest. I had to learn to twirl a flag with my right hand even though I am left-handed.

Maurcia and I remained friends for many, many years. Her daughter is my Goddaughter and my daughter is hers, though neither of us has met the other's child. We used to write letters. For some reason she never gave me an email address which would have made keeping up with her a lot easier. She went on to become a nurse and moved to South Jersey. I haven't heard from her in a couple of years.

My boyfriend for two years was Alex. He had the most beautiful, girlish eyelashes I've ever seen. He was a track star. He was funny, well-liked and popular. And he picked me out of all the other girls in the world. We went to the senior prom together. I used to see him whenever I visited. We were friends for a few years.

He asked me to marry him. He knew I was involved with someone and wouldn't say yes. He knew that I lived in Germany and wasn't planning to move back home. He knew that asking me in front of a group of family and friends would make the situation worse. Still, he went for it and I said no. After that, there wasn't much more to talk about. Our friendship ended and that was that.

The most famous graduate of VHS Class of '88 was Wyclef Jean, though he wasn't called that back then. He was just plain Jean. We weren't friends but we hung in the same circles. He was really into performing even back then.

I was great friends with his cousin Sam, who was my academic competitor. I always wondered if Sam became a preacher like his father. If I ever run into Wyclef Jean, I'll ask him about Sam.

I don't think there is a reunion planned. If there is, no one invited me. That may be because they don't have a clue where to find me. There is probably a rumor about how I left home and never came back. Can anyone guess that I've gone to Texas?

Mrs. Jones is a lady on Hudson Street

Someone told me that if you approach an American 35 to 45 years old, and say 'Conjunction Junction,' their response will invariably be 'What's Your Function?' That's right, we grew up on School House Rock. And not the crummy, cheesy 80s version of the Saturday morning cartoon commercial/educational series; we had the groovy, catchy clips of the 1970s.

My mother didn't worry about us watching mindless hours of cartoons because she knew that somewhere between commercials for Lucky Charms and Hot Wheels, we were going to learn something. And she was right.

School House Rock snuck in some heavy learning shrouded in funky lyrics and hip characters. I learned about the Electoral College and what a bill had to go through to become a law. I learned about women's suffrage and how people from all over the world came to the United States to create a great big melting pot. I learned that a noun is a person, place or thing. I learned that you could shop for adverbs at Lolly's.

I knew a cache of cool songs like 'Electricity, Electricity' and 'Verb! That's What's Happening.' Though many decades have passed, I still know many of the words to most of those songs.

I got to meet Rufus Xavier Sarsaparilla and his sister, Rafaella Gabriela Sarsaparilla. I took a trip to the Statue of Liberty. I found that if I ever needed help with verbs, I could turn to a bulky black dude wearing a cape. I discovered that three is a magic number.

If I needed an interjection, I could use Aw! Eeek! Rats! and Wow!! because an interjection starts a sentence off right. I could conjugate verbs like a pro. I could rattle off multiplication tables like a math whiz. Oh yeah! I was good. I even thought it would be great if I could skate a figure eight.

I am indebted to School House Rock for molding my malleable, little, unsuspecting brain. Considering the entire collection of SHR commercials, the creators put an enormous amount of complex information out into the world. And we schoolchildren of the 1970s ate it up like giant bowls of corn flakes and powdered milk. We honestly had no idea that we were being covertly educated.

I outgrew SHR in the 1980s, just about the time when the series started tumbling downhill like a victim of gravity. I don't know if kids got wiser or the suits took over production but folksy was replaced by quasi-sophistication – better graphics, polished songs and obvious teaching. This was School House Rock's downfall. Saturday morning started to seem more like school and none of us kids wanted to learn.

Or maybe we just grew up.

Today, you can rent SHR DVDs or watch them from YouTube. It's fun to reminisce. My favorites are from the Grammar Rock collection. I rented the complete series last year and watched it all in a single evening. My daughter got out of bed at about midnight and asked, 'What are you singing?!'

I said, "Well, it's a long, long journey but I'm going to get you there if you're very careful."

Adrian Jackson is a freelance writer in Beeville, Texas. She grew up during the heyday of educational television with shows like Fat Albert, The Electric Company, Zoom and those much-loved School House Rock commercials.

I won't pass poverty on to my daughter

I rented an old movie last week. It was made in the 1970s. The story was about a single mother with six kids. I have seen the movie at least a half dozen times. It was very popular when I was a kid. I was struck by how poor the family was. They lived in a small apartment with a single bathroom. Some of the kids shared beds and one slept on the couch. That's how it was in the 70s.

I remember my mother's apartment. We lived on the first floor of a three-story house owned by my grandparents. Even by today's standards we had a pretty large apartment, but we only had three bedrooms. I shared a room with two sisters. I shared a bed with one. I shared a bed until I was a teenager. By the time I got my own room, there were only two of us left at home and I was a senior in high school.

I don't remember us being poor, though we couldn't have had much money. Back then if a father left home he took his paycheck with him and there was little legal recourse for the children left behind. My mom raised us alone. She earned a good salary, but even today, one paycheck doesn't stretch far in a house of five.

I remember getting new clothes before school started. That was the only time I got new clothes. Mom shopped at a department store and bought pants three sizes too big so we'd have room to grow. She used to patch our jeans before we put them on to shore up the knees. Some of my 'new' clothes were my sisters' hand-me-downs. We had 'school' clothes and 'play' clothes and we knew better than to get caught playing in what we had worn to school.

Today's kids live a very different life than I did. I have one child, but even if I had three more, their lives would be markedly different than mine was. My daughter's father lives far away, but his physical absence has not extracted him from our daily lives. My daughter has always had her own room. She sleeps in a queen-sized loft bed. She's always had the master bedroom with the biggest closets filled with toys and clothes.

She has disposable income and a check card to access her account. She spends her money on toys, clothes, teddy bears and DVDs. I try to say little about how she decides to spend her own money. When I was her age I only got money on holidays and that gift was usually followed by a trip to the store.

My daughter has her own electronic equipment. She has a portable DVD player, a laptop, an iPod, a camera and two stereos. She has a microscope, a telescope, a Wii console, a karaoke machine and a cell phone. She has roller blades, Heelies, a scooter and a bike. These all belong to her and she doesn't have to share with anyone else, including me.

It sounds extravagant on paper, but this is what kids today have. She is no different than most of her friends. Her life is very different than my childhood was. In some ways, I am pleased to be able to provide a better life for her than I had. In other ways, I wonder if not having to struggle, scrimp or save will have some detrimental effect on her years from now when she'll have to manage her own household. I don't know where I stack up against other parents who grew up in the 1970s like me. I guess time will tell if any of us have made the right choices.

My life in decades

My first ten years made up the decade of enlightenment. My mother was committed to enriching our lives with literature and culture. We attended festivals, concerts, shows and frequented galleries and museums. It helped that New York City was just a train ride away.

I got my own library card when I was six. I was allowed to check out books without my mother's assistance. We took weekly trips to the library which was within walking distance of our home. My mother challenged us to read beyond our grade level and in doing so, I learned to read well.

My older sisters took music and dance lessons. I didn't but I was encouraged to do what I loved. Even before I could write, I made up stories to entertain myself. My mother thought I was weird but was kind enough not to say so until I was much older.

My next ten years made up the decade of appeasement. My mother left home a month before I turned 11 and we went to live with my grandfather and his second wife. It was a hard decade, marred by alcoholism and apathy. We were not encouraged to grow or explore. I did what I could to be the best at everything in attempts to gain attention and affection.

We were expected to do well in school. I excelled out of the need to be recognized for being a good daughter. Much of what I did was centered on distinguishing me from others at home and in school. I graduated in the top ten of my class and earned four scholarships for college.

I was very actively involved in school. I was shy, but knew I didn't want to be in that shell forever. I put myself into situations that forced me to speak up. I joined the debate team. I ran for class vice president (and lost). I became a cheerleader (varsity). I did the homecoming pageant (won Miss Vailsburg High School 1988).

I grew out of my teens with a lot of emotional scars but it was a time of personal success. I have many happy memories of that time and I discovered my inner strength.

My 20s was the decade of travel. I lived in Europe for 11 years. I went to many, many countries by car, bus and plane. I had a job that required me to travel to five countries on a regular basis. I had friends from all over the world and many of them were multi-cultural and spoke more than one language. I had a great love affair. I lived in a condo. I was very sophisticated.

Even after the birth of my daughter in 1997, I continued to travel a lot. I tell people that she'd been to more places in utero than most people have been to in a lifetime. At no point in her life did my daughter slow me down from enjoying my time in Europe. I've passed my love of adventure on to her.

My 30s make up the decade of education. I went back to college in 2000. I quit my job, returned to the U.S., and spent two years earning an associate's degree. I graduated and went back to work, but continued the commitment to my education. I earned a bachelor's degree in 2006. I am now working on a graduate degree that can lead to a Ph.D. if I stick with the program. I think I'll finish the current degree before the decade ends.

My commitment to education extends to my daughter, who knows that she has to at least catch up to my level of education. That girl's got her work cut out for her. I'm an over-achiever.

Three years from now, I'll turn 40. I have no idea what the 2010s will hold for me or how I will look back and define that decade. The possibilities are endless and I'm excited to see what will happen next.

How does my garden grow?

I am a plant killer. My photo is on the wall of every nursery and florist in America. I am on the top ten list. No one in their right mind would ever sell me a living plant.

It is no surprise that I have scant few plants, alive or plastic, in my home. I have bamboo stalks that are idiot proof but I killed one of them a few months ago. The other two are on notice. I have five bamboo stalks at work. They are beautiful. I can only attribute this to the fact that there are witnesses around.

I live in a beautiful neighborhood. There are all manner of flowers, bushes, manicured lawns and irrigation systems. Many neighbors have gardeners with motorized vehicles tend their expansive lawns. My house is the one with the brown squares in front. What I call a lawn, you might call a big weed patch. I'm the one with the yard that is bringing property values down. I let my grass grow about three feet before I have it mowed.

I'm sure there is a deep psychological reason I am against putting forth the work required to grow anything green. It may be rooted in years and years of being pulled out of bed on Saturday mornings to mow, rake, trim, pull and clip the front lawn of my childhood home. It was not fun. It was a chore. My grandfather, unlike me, took great pride in his front yard. We had beautiful azaleas and something called Kentucky Bluegrass (which, by the way, comes up green). He liked bushes. Our front yard was bordered by waist-high hedges. It was very pretty, but a lot of work. He didn't mind. I think he looked forward to this weekend work.

He had a vegetable garden in the back. Granddaddy always grew tomatoes. He would switch off plants with a neighbor, who was equally successful with tomatoes. My grandfather moved his crop around every year. Sometimes we'd get residual tomatoes from the previous patch.

One of my best memories is of his brown knurly fingers delicately rolling a fat, red tomato around the palm of his hand. He would stand there for hours talking about his vegetables. I think he was trying to teach me something, but I didn't listen.

He'd line up tomatoes on the kitchen windowsill to ripen. We had so many during the summer that we'd eat them for snacks. We regularly had a surplus of onions, carrots, squash, zucchini, beans, potatoes and peas. We'd have an occasional eggplant and a strawberry or two each year. We always joked about my grandfather's gardening. He, like me, was a city kid, born and raised in Newark, New Jersey. I never understood his love of gardening because it seems so incongruous to his nature. In hind sight, I wish I had paid attention just once so that I knew something about how to make a garden grow.

Since I have a large lot, I feel ecologically-obligated to grow something, but what can someone like me plant without killing it? I'd like to grow something that I can eat because I don't see the practicality of flowers (though my neighbors might appreciate the effort). I like the smell of herbs and peppers. What can I put into the ground, never water, never tend, that grows beautifully? Please don't suggest cacti, because I've killed a few of those too.

Young life lost to shot to the head

Christopher Bizilj died last month of a self-inflicted gunshot wound. What makes this story unique is that the shooter was an eight-year-old, the gun was an Uzi, and he was under the supervision of two adults – a shooting expert and the boy's father. He lost his life in a tragic mindless act of adult stupidity.

Now, before you get your shackles up, let me state that I am not opposed to owning guns. I don't own a gun but I have shot one. I've also gone to a couple of gun shows. They were actually more historical memorabilia shows where guns were on display than actual gun shows. I've considered owning a gun but at this time it doesn't fit my lifestyle.

The issue with Bizilj's death is that two adults watched this horror unfold at a gun show filled with perceivably responsible adults. Somewhere in the gun expert's mind, it was a good idea to allow an eight-year-old to handle a fully loaded sub-machine gun. *Fully loaded machine gun.* As any mother can tell you an eight-year-old can barely handle a basketball or a glass of milk let alone a machine gun. Why then, would anyone allow an eight-year-old to handle a weapon that he could quickly lose control of? An Uzi is not a Daisy air rifle.

The other adult was the boy's father, who not only thought it was a good idea to take an eight-year-old to a machine gun expo but also thought it was perfectly okay to allow the kid to shoot a sub-machine gun. What was he thinking? Was he thinking at all?

The child's dad said the accident was a true mystery to him. He said he thought the gun expert had his hands on the gun. The father stood about ten feet away from the boy when the gun flipped backward and let one off into the kid's head. That shot was the cause of the boy's death.

The father later called his young son an adventurer and outdoorsman. I say that the boy didn't have time to grow into those roles; his life was so quickly snuffed out.

I've never shot an Uzi or even a shotgun, but I know enough about guns to know that even the slightest recoil is too much for a small boy.

I'm curious to know what gun enthusiasts feel about this story. Is it normal to expect a child to be able to handle a sub-machine gun? There are clips of other young children handling the same gun. Is this kind of shooting fairly common or is this rare and disturbing?

I think kids can be exposed to guns like anything else – with moderation and safety. Bizilj should have been years away from handling a gun of that magnitude. There are many guns out there suitable for someone his age with the proper supervision. Just because he wanted to shoot it, doesn't mean that his father should have given his permission. It seems to me that the child would have survived being told no. As a parent, I could rail all day long about the stupid decisions that result in the injury or death of a child. But at the end of this story Christopher Bizilj is still dead. May he rest in peace.

Reporters mishandle a tragic story

John Travolta's son Jett died last week. He was 16 years old. The story of his tragic death made headlines right away, as it would if any top-tiered celebrity was involved.

Shortly after I heard about Travolta's death, a Bahaman man, high up in the government, claiming to be a friend, gave an account of how the family was grieving. He went on for a while and at first I thought he was the family spokesperson. But, in listening to his words, I realized that he was probably a neighbor or someone who'd casually met the family. He was no friend. A friend would never engage in scrutinizing a mourning family or speculating about a death, within 24 hours of the tragedy, on national television.

Another man, the emergency medical technician, gave a moment-by-moment account of what took place once he arrived on the scene. He shared some intimate details of very private moments.

The next day, a Bahaman medical official, not the one who performed the autopsy, got a top spot on the morning news. He spent a great deal of the interview admitting that he had nothing to do with the autopsy and pontificating his no-nothing opinion. He bloviated for a good ten minutes to a reporter who was no less excited to cover the story than a National Enquirer cub reporter.

After Mr. Blah-de-blah was done, another reporter introduced an American expert guest, a doctor of something. She voiced her opinion based on the fact that she's had no contact with the family and was no less than 1,000 miles from anyone with any sort of knowledge of what may have happened. She, like doctors on television seem to do a lot these days, rebutted what had been speculated as the cause of the boy's death stating that it is just not possible to have happened as it was stated to have. Being a doctor of something, she probably does have the credentials to medically speculate. But, the next thing she did was expound on her theory of the boy's medical health having never examined him in life or death.

I thought to myself, 'How dare she?! Who does she think she is to express an opinion about this tragedy?' Truth be told, she wasn't at fault; the reporter all but gave her a microphone and a stage. She gormandized the doctor's position that the Travoltas were at fault for their son's death.

As a clip of a crate being loaded into a car, presumably headed to the airport, rolled in the background, the two women speculated that it was all staged and the boy's body had already been cremated. The reporter and guest debated whether or not the American media had a right to the autopsy report, against Bahaman law.

And therein lies the problem. Reporters, trying to outdo other news shows with who can get the most information out the fastest, forget that it's not just a story; it is the death of a human being. There is a family in mourning and compassion is called for. Jett Travolta died tragically and everything else is irrelevant.

As the story segued, the weatherman quietly said, 'At the end of the day, a family has lost their son. Our condolences to the Travolta family.' His statement summed up all that the story should have been.

Ya want keffiyeh with that doughnut?

Rachael Ray landed into a steaming pot of hot java recently when ultra-conservative columnist Michelle Malkin accused her of being jihadi chic.

Ray, in a Dunkin' Donuts commercial, donned what some might call a paisley scarf, but Malkin quickly recognized as a signal of support for Islamic extremism. Malkin hoped that Ray chose the scarf out of ignorance but suspected that it was a non-too-subtle message to terrorists. A shout-out, if you will.

Seriously? This is Rachael Ray we are talking about. She's about as controversial as Gidget in a two-piece bathing suit. As a matter of fact, Ray does have a Gidget, girl-next-door, America's sweetheart personality.

If you don't know who Rachael Ray is, as is apparent in Malkin's case, or you've never watched any of her shows – 30-Minute Meals, $40 a Day, Rachael Ray Show, Rachael Ray's Tasty Travels or the short-lived Inside Dish you may be tempted to give Malkin room to rant. If you've never read her magazine, Everyday with Rachael Ray, or one of her dozens of cookbooks, you may look at the scarf and wonder if it is possible.

But if you know anything about Ray you know this is both ridiculous and stupid. It is, however, indicative of everything wrong with Malkin's brand of writing. Her work is inflammatory and viral. Malkin caused an uproar years ago during a California book signing when she spoke out in favor of the internment of Japanese-Americans during WWII. More recently, she called Chris Matthews of MSNBC a 'spittle-flecked caveman.' I'm no fan of Matthews but that's hitting below the belt.

Basically, Malkin is a right-wing tangent ranter. What makes her viral is that she has a blog which means that she can reach more people around the world than her column ever could in print alone. She can also control the message coming from her website with the authority to accept or reject reader responses.

So if Malkin wants to believe that Ray is a terrorist sympathizer, she can perpetuate that position in her own little stratosphere. And those who find validity in her argument can congregate around her like misbegotten planets.

In Malkin's defense, she does allow conflicting comments to be posted. If you go to her blog and review this particular topic, you will see that even some of Malkin's fans believe that this one is way out in right field. Ray is a bundle of energy wrapped up in a small body with a mega-watt smile. She's the kind of person who hugs everybody. I've never met her, but I bet if I showed up at her door she'd invite me in and cook something for me. Knowing that, it is believable that the scarf was just a scarf.

An Islamic extremist? I think not. Could a terrorist make Bacon Wrapped Blue Cheese Stuffed Chicken with Green Beans and Smashed Potatoes in 30 minutes?

Adrian Jackson is a freelance writer in Beeville, Texas. She is not a terrorist.

What's wrong with the Suleman 8?

There is much speculation surrounding the octuplets born to a 33-year-old single mother. It seems that everyone has an opinion, but do we have the right to one? I think the fact that the mother is making rounds on the morning show circuit certainly means that she has willingly opened her doors to scrutiny. So, I think it's okay to step in.

I'm not genuinely firm on any part of the controversy. My opinions vary as I look at issues from different perspectives. I try to avoid making sweeping statements for or against any part of this odd story because it is a unique and nuanced situation.

I think it is medically irresponsible to give birth to eight children at once. I don't blame this on science. It's no one's fault that all the embryos took. I don't blame it on religion. It is a gift and a miracle – a reason to rejoice. I blame it on a society that is addicted to super-sizing everything even if that means implanting eight embryos to increase the likelihood of success. I blame it on a doctor who convinced this mother that eight was better than four.

I think that a woman has the right to make decisions for herself without legislators hovering over her uterus. On the other hand, I think we have to protect unborn children from stupid decisions made by feckless parents. We can't force embryonic limits on parents but this case is certainly a good argument for it.

It seems that we glorify multiple births by making families celebrities. We lavish them with attention; we give them gifts; we photograph them and track their progress through the years. We build them houses and give them their own TV shows. I always think of the Dionne Quints who were taken from their parents and made to grow up in front of the public like zoo animals. Celebrity seems to bring in big bucks but at what cost to children?

I have no criticism for someone who wants to have 14 children. I think families ought to have as many children as they desire and I don't think that their income should be a considerable factor in their decision. What I mean is as long as parents can care for their children, who are we to tell them when to stop having them? But if parents enter into this situation, knowing that they will never have the resources to meet the basic needs of the children, you have to question their motive and logic.

In this case, the mother appears to have financial problems. This concerns me. These babies are preemies and have already received millions of dollars of medical care. They will continue to need more than average medical attention since it is very likely that some will have physical and developmental issues throughout their lives. These babies might turn out to be a special burden on California taxpayers; a problem because it diminishes funding for other families in need. That said, it doesn't mean that I think that poor families are less deserving of children than rich ones or that they are less able to manage 14 children. I know that neither of those is true. I'm saying that a little less selfishness and a little more financial planning could have saved the taxpayers, the hospital and the family a lot of money.

Nadya Suleman said she will depend on her friends, family and church for assistance. It is great to have a support network in place. She'll need one. But what happens when people stop coming by? What will happen when people turn their attention elsewhere? What is Suleman's plan then?

There are 14 young children headed into a turbulent life. They need our prayers every day.

Bertinelli is not your typical cover model

Valerie Bertinelli in a bikini at her age? You go girl!

Bertinelli, a longtime actress known for her cherubic face, showed off her newly trimmed hot body on the cover of People Magazine. With a commitment to being spokesperson for Jenny Craig (on the heels of Kirstie Alley who has gained back half of her 75 lost pounds) and the help of a personal trainer, Bertinelli is happy with the results.

Just the fact that 48-year-old Bertinelli had the guts to slip into a bikini makes me admire her. I think Bertinelli is comfortable in her own skin and the abs and delts add an extra boost to her confidence. She looks great and inspires me to set a bikini goal.

I wore my last bikini when I was three years old. As a child, my mother didn't buy us bikinis. I don't remember if they were out of fashion or just inappropriate for little girls but I did not have one. When I became a teenager, I was too self-conscious to wear a bikini. I was gangly and awkward.

As a young woman, I avoided wearing a bikini for the same reasons. I was more confident than I had been as a teenager, but still too timid to bare that much skin in public. I wish I'd had the option of wearing surfer shorts or those mix-and-match suits that are popular today.

Someone told me that I should just get over myself and get a bikini before it was too late. She was right. I gained weight over the next 20 years and now I wouldn't dream of wearing a bikini or any two-piece swim outfit. I think my not wearing a bikini is a public service at this point.

If I lost 50 pounds now, like Bertinelli, I would certainly slip (or stuff) myself into a bikini though I'd need to shed quite a few more before I'd willingly wear one to a beach. I think that I am more confident about who I am and more comfortable in my own skin than ever but I've got some growing up to do yet. I am working toward the point of not caring about what people think or say about me and that is liberating, especially in Bikiniland.

That's the secret, isn't it? It's confidence.

I fell in love with the late Chris Farley when he did that Chippendale's bit with Patrick Swayze on Saturday Night Live. Farley, the kind of brilliant comedian who would do anything, anything for a laugh, ripped off his shirt and gyrated to the music like a pro, making him one of the sexiest men alive. The guts it took to dance shirtless like a great big jiggly mess, next to Swayze no less, made him a comic god. If you've never seen that clip, I suggest you watch it on the internet. You'll laugh until you pee and fall head over heels for the fat guy in tights like millions of Americans did that night it aired.

If I had Farley's gumption, I would buy a bikini tomorrow in a devil-may-care frenzy but I don't. I am more like the Bertinellis of the world – lose 50 pounds, tone up an additional three weeks and smile for my big cover. You rock, Val!

Take a hike, Heloise!

I've got some home tips for my readers that will rival anything Heloise has to say.

A few months ago, someone told me that if you wrap celery in aluminum foil it will retain its crunch forever. It sounded suspicious to me, but having both celery and foil at home, I decided to give it a try. Well, wonder of all wonders, it works! I can keep celery fresh for weeks. It is just as crispy three weeks later than it was the day I bought it. This is revolutionary. I wish I could remember who give me this fridge tip because I'd like to send her a year's supply of foil.

Alton Brown of the television show Good Eats says you should buy an avocado when it is firm unless you plan to use it right away. He recommends that you put hard avocados in a brown paper bag and leave the bag out in a cool, dry place. They will ripen in a few days. Here is the revolutionary part: Once they ripen, put them in the refrigerator. The cold air will halt the ripening process, producing perfectly ripened avocados that will store for a week or two. If you just toss the hard avocados in the fridge as is, the halted ripening process will result in avocados that will never soften.

A refrigerator tip that I've used for years involved onions and bell peppers. I buy multiple varieties of onions, slice them and toss them into a freezer bag. The variety adds a complex layer of flavor to meals and the onions keep forever. Of course, these onions are not crunchy, so they won't work well in a salad, but if they are going to be cooked, they ready for the pan.

The cost of bell peppers goes up and down with the seasons. I buy lots of them when the green ones go down to about 50 cents. Red, orange and yellow seldom dip below 75 cents but I keep my eyes on them. Since I like the variety that mixed peppers bring to a dish, I buy all four colors, cut them up and store them in a freezer bag like the onions. Whenever I want to add bell pepper to a dish, the peppers are not only ready for the pot, they are also very colorful. When I buy more, I just add them to the same bag. Brilliant, I know.

I mop my floors before I sweep them. The mop pulls dirt out of hard-to-reach places. It also picks up a lot of the dirt making sweeping easier. When the floor dries, I go over it with a broom. Sweeping is much easier and faster when half the work is done for you.

A tip for new moms: Watch out for end-of-season sales. When your child is an infant, buy him or her a big trunk. Fill that trunk with clothes when prices at your favorite store are slashed. Buy off-season clothes in larger sizes. For example: if your baby wears 6-9-months today, buy 18-months on sale and pull them out of the trunk when your baby grows into them next year. You will find that you can get very nice pieces at almost any store for less than five dollars each, especially holiday outfits, swimsuits, shorts and pajamas.

    A tip for moms of teens: If you have a fashion-forward teen, invest in only a few designer pieces. Your kid can mix and match designer wear with department store brands. If your teen is wearing a Hollister Co. Sunset Cliffs t-shirt, who cares what kind of jeans he or she has paired it with? Oh, and another hint about mall stores: the sale stuff is usually located at the front center of the store (to entice passers-by). The more expensive stuff is located at the back, so if you must go, pressure your kid to make a selection right away and not wander his or her way to the high dollar section.

I am a filing disaster

I am generally a well-organized person. I live by deadlines. I shred old documents and I can show you my tax returns going back to 1992. I pride myself on my ability to bring order to chaos. It is listed as a skill on my resume.

So, imagine my surprise to find that I've completely lost my daughter's immunization records. I don't have a clue when exactly I lost them so the prospect of figuring out where they are is pretty slim. I looked in all of the regular places – special boxes, drawers and folders reserved for very important papers. I've looked in irregular places – under the bed and on the computer desk. I've come up empty handed every time.

Immunization records are those top-tiered documents that are virtually impossible to replace, especially if they were created on two different continents. My daughter got half of her shots in Germany and the other half in Texas so her official records are a compilation of the two. They do not entirely exist in a database like most children born in this state.

I was lucky enough to get a copy of the records from my daughter's school. Here's to grade school administrators who organize the records of hundreds of children each year with their mad filing skills. They put small-time filers like me to shame.

While trying to find the records, I stumbled upon a deed to property that I bought almost a year ago. I had looked for those papers for months before completely giving up so I was glad to have them. I also found my old address book. This is good timing since Christmas is just around the corner and I'll need the addresses to mail cards.

I am a tactile learner. I learn by touching, feeling and turning things over in my hands. I store memories based on tangible things – where I was, what I was doing, how I was dressed, what something smelled like. If I can just remember something about the day the records left their former location, I can recall where they are today. If only I could remember something, anything.

I'm the sort of person who always put things in the same spot to ensure that they never get misplaced. My keys always go on top of the chest to the left of the front door. My eyeglasses go on the floor on the left side of my bed. This simple system keeps me from having to recall. I can find things out of habit which is important in my hectic life. There is a place for those records but they are not there.

It turns out that even though I think I am organized and I am rather snobbish about my superior organizing skills, I am in fact, a paperwork disaster. Shame on me. I've got some filing to do.

It ain't easy going green

I am going to reduce my imprint on the Earth by limiting my use of plastic bags.

When I lived in Germany, I either brought my own grocery bags to the store or paid for the ones I used. In most of Europe, this shopping tradition is normal. It is quite ordinary to walk out of the store with a cart full of groceries and not a bag in sight. It took some getting used to this but once I did it really wasn't an inconvenience. I usually stashed a few cloth bags in the trunk of my car and bagged when I got out of the store. Some people used collapsible plastic boxes to transport groceries. Others just took the cart home.

When I first moved to Texas, I shopped at a grocery store that offered paper or plastic. I initially asked for paper, but as time went by I slipped into a plastic habit. It is hard to be ecologically friendly when the bad ones have the neat, easy-to-carry handles.

So, I used plastic bags like a glutton. I even double-bagged. I told myself that I would recycle the bags so I stockpiled them in my pantry. As you can guess, I never actually recycled the bags. I just stored them until I couldn't stand it anymore and then crammed them all in the trash. I did reuse them when I could. There are lots of uses for those grocery sacks but after a while there are more sacks than uses.

Now, I've decided to go green. Not Ed Begley green, but a small step in the right direction. If we all just do our part we can change the world. If I keep telling myself that maybe I'll actually make a difference.

I bought some cloth bags from the grocery store. They only cost 99 cents each. They are green and have a hard plastic bottom, so that they open up into a rectangle. I've already started using them.

I went to the store the other day and asked the cashier not to bag my groceries. She nodded, handed me the first two items and started bagging again. 'No,' I said. 'I don't need bags. I'll just put them in the cart.' She nodded, but gave me the look. You know the one. It is the same look the lady in line behind me gave the cashier when she thought I wasn't looking. I filled up my cart and headed out the store. I got a strange look from another store employee who must have thought I'd stolen a cart full of eggs, cabbage and soy milk. She didn't stop me though. She just gave me the look.

I got out to my car, opened the trunk and filled up my green bags with the groceries. A family of passers-by gave me the look. I smiled.

I'm going green. What do I care of these unenlightened Neanderthals? I'm just doing my part.

When I went to a bookstore at the mall the next day, I refused the bag and carried my books out of the store. You know what? I didn't miss those handles at all. It turns out that the books fit nicely under my arm.

I'm off to a great, green start.

I'm still green

I wrote a column a few months ago about going green. I made a commitment to using reusable bags at the grocery store instead of the plastic throwaways. I'm still at it and it has changed my life!

When I first started using cloth bags I got funny looks. Mostly from cashiers. Over time either they got used to seeing me whip out my bright green bags or there were so many people using cloth bags that it was no longer an odd thing to do. I don't know. Who cares? The point is that now cashiers and baggers smile when I tell them that I've brought my own bags or they take the cloth bags from me and pack them.

One downside is that I occasionally forget to bring the bags into the store. Normally, I just turn back around and retrieve them from the car but once I didn't realize that I didn't have them until I got to the register. I got into an argument with the cashier who refused to let me leave the store with my unsacked groceries. As if she has the right to tell me what to do with groceries I'd already paid for. Maybe she does. Maybe it's a store policy. I don't know. Who cares? On that day I bested her and walked out with no bags. I popped open my trunk, pulled out my cloth sacks and loaded my stuff in them.

Another downside is that we have very few plastic bags around the house these days. They are great for trash, carrying the dog's pooper scooper and using as a bonnet to condition my hair. I've had to go out and purchase plastic caps for the latter chore.

The upside to reusable bags is that I can fit into one bag what was previously packed into five bags. I seldom come out of the store with more than two bags. This means that I make fewer trips between the car and the house to unload. I can carry more articles in a bag without the worry of the bag ripping or the plastic cutting into my hand. I can carry bags lower to the ground so that the weigh is better distributed and they don't seem as heavy. I can unpack groceries without having to pick up dozens of white bags strewn over the kitchen floor.

Impact on the environment or not, I love the reusable bags. I take them everywhere. I use them for everything. I try to be sensitive by coupling the right bags with the right stores.

Not that I've completely given up on plastic. That was never my intention. I still use plastic store bags for cleaning products. I don't want to risk spillage. I still use the white bags for meat. I don't want to risk cross-contamination. I still use freezer bags and garbage bags.

But I've taken a step that I feel good about and can live with. I'm proud of myself.

The next thing I'd like to tackle is gas. I can't make a big impact statement like buying a hybrid car or riding my bike to work, but I can do small things. I've already started walking to the grocery store. I strap on a backpack with my cloth bags and a waterproof jacket inside and walk to the store once a week. I buy only what I can carry. I tack on a few other errands like checking my mailbox and stopping by the video store so that I can make the most of the trip. I won't singlehandedly bring down the price at the pump, but maybe over six months I'll save myself a full tank of gas. I don't know. Who cares? I'll get a little exercise and help the environment.

If Longoria uses reusable bags, you should too

I'm no great fan of actress Eva Longoria, but I love her new reusable bag campaign. It's an eco-conscious career move for her.

I know that we consumers are inundated with calls to 'Go Green' and it's difficult to know whether or not our personal decisions are truly making an impact on the world. We want to be responsible stewards of this planet, but we don't want to waste time on insignificant actions that change nothing in the big picture. That's why it is so important to get on board with reusable bags.

It is such a small commitment -- a promise to use cloth, canvas or any reusable bag in the place of those plastic ones that the stores provide. It only requires that you build up a collection of bags and that you remember to bring them when you shop. The first one is easy. You can buy bags everywhere, including the one with Longoria's signature. They usually cost under $1. Some are more expensive; some are free. Last year, we got two free bags for Earth Day (April 22). The latter commitment takes a bit of work. It will take a while to get used to grabbing those bags before you walk away from your car. That part can be frustrating, but you'll get over it soon enough.

I have bags from Wal-Mart, HEB, Walgreens, Half-Priced Bookstore, Barnes and Nobles, IKEA and World Market. I've gotten into shopping for bags now. The canvas bags are the best, but the plastic ones are much bigger. My Home Depot bags have a neat locking system and they're orange.

I keep bags in my trunk and pull them out as needed. When I'm done, I hang them on the front door so I'll remember to take them back out to the car.

If you don't like the idea of carrying around a sack emblazoned with a retailer's logo or are just too trendy for cheap bags, don't worry. There are designer totes out there. Naturally, they cost about $20 each, but they are of a higher quality and usually look nicer. I have a great big beach bag that I shop with sometimes. It is practically bottomless.

Why do you think retailers are on board with the bags? Because it is free advertising. Because they save money by purchasing fewer store bags. Because the parking lots and the community at large are cleaner when there are fewer bags flying around. Because consumers appreciate retailers who are doing something to make our world a better place.

Did you know that plastic bags are not biodegradable? They break apart (not down) and release toxins into soil and waterways. Did you know that millions of animals die each year from eating plastic bags mistaken for food? Did you know that plastic bags rank in the top 12 of items discovered during coastline cleanups?

One million bags are used every minute, according to Reusablebags.com. Now is the time to be a part of the solution. If Eva Longoria thinks reusable bags are cool (and you know you know people who know her) and I think reusable bags are cool, then why aren't you using reusable bags?

Adrian Jackson is a resident of Bee County. She committed to using reusable bags one year ago and has found that while the change wasn't easy, it continues to be well worth it.

Author baffled by the change

I have a colleague who had a gender reassignment. As much as I respect this person, I can't help but think that this is an extremely narcissistic act.

This person is married with children. I don't know what ages the children are but even if they are adults, they have to deal with the emotional damage that goes with having a birth father, a Dad, who is now a woman. Even if the kids are supportive and have been able to take this evolution one step at a time, it is still a ticking bomb on the kitchen table. And no matter how Hollywood tries to glorify transmogrification, I can imagine it wreaks havoc on sons and daughters leaving more carnage than a Terminator.

My philosophy on sexual identity is: Pick a team. When you are a rookie or a free agent you can pinch hit for the other team all you want but once spouses and children are involved, you've signed a contract and you stay where you play.

She explained her decision to make the change in a very heartfelt letter. She was very open about what she went through for years, living in a body that didn't seem to belong to her.

The process, clinically, takes a long time. It's not like he showed up for work one day in a skirt. Truth be told, I guess it was kind of like that to those who've known him for years regardless of how subtle the changes were.

It takes a lot of guts to go through this kind of change in front of your co-workers. I think it would be easier if it coincided with a job change and a move to a new city. That way, you could at least bypass the awkward stage. People would only know you as you are not as you were.

It takes even more guts to spring this sort of thing on your spouse. On the one hand, I think, his wife must have realized years ago that something wasn't quite right. I don't know how he expressed his desire to be a woman before he decided to make physical changes, but his wife must have noticed something. It is a tragedy for her because she certainly wouldn't have entered a marriage with the intention of this outcome, would she? I don't think marriage vows extend that far into that territory.

She has remained with him throughout this ordeal. They are still together though it's been almost a year since the surgery. And even though he is who he always was and that is probably the appeal for her, he is not, by any definition, a husband. She lost her husband. She has to deal with that.

She also has to deal with the fact that she is in a relationship with a woman. Does that make her a lesbian? Did she consent to becoming a lesbian? Does he have the right to ask that of her? It seems to me that if she had intended to be a lesbian, she would have married a woman in the first place. And the fact that she is a de facto lesbian doesn't diminish much of the plain truth.

The children now have two mothers and no father. The wife has a girlfriend and no husband. The gender-reassigned colleague has made a personal decision but the aftershocks will reverberate through his family for years to come.

One child is enough for me

I believe that God doesn't give you more than you can handle. And He has seen fit to bestow upon me only one child.

I say this because I watch other people with multiple children and wonder how they maintain their sanity. My oldest sister has seven children. There has't been a single day of quiet, calm or organization in her home in more than 25 years. I've always told my sister that if I were her, I would lock myself in my room and let the children raise themselves.

I used to dread calling my sister when her kids were little. The conversation was interrupted by the background sounds of music, noise and constant chatter. My sister's side of the conversation was stilted with interjections like 'No, you can't have that' 'Can't you see I'm on the phone' and 'Leave your brother alone.' For me, single with no children, it was exhausting. Couldn't she find a quiet place to talk? Couldn't the kids leave her alone long enough for a phone conversation?

Today, her youngest child is 16 and she is finishing up the child-rearing years of her life. She has come through it beautifully with well-adjusted, college-educated adults who've left home (but are known to return frequently) and three teenagers on the cusp of striking out on their own.

My older sister has three daughters. It is incredible to watch three sisters who are completely opposite as though they are strangers forced to live together in the same house and share the same parents. These three girls, ages five to 10, are in no way alike and their differences give rise to hissy-fits and battles. There is a lot of whining, yelling, crying and complaining in my sister's house. Having grown up with three sisters, I don't remember us being so mean to each other.

When I wanted my daughter to experience what it was like to have sisters, I packed her up and dropped her off at my sister's for the summer. She now appreciates what it means to have her own room, her own things and no one to have to share with. I'm sure my daughter would agree that while I enjoy spending time with my sister's family, I am ever grateful that my house is much quieter.

My youngest sister has three sons, ages six and under. Her boys are a rough and tumble bunch. They fight over toys and attention. Their personalities are different and don't always mesh. I think her oldest son would prefer if he were an only child.

I've taken to watching the reality television show Jon and Kate Plus 8. If you've never heard of the show, it is about a couple who have twin daughters and sextuplets (a three/three split). Their babies are three and their older girls are seven. I like to watch this show because despite the noise, fighting and crying, the household is better organized than mine. The parents treat each child as an individual and they all seem to be happy. The parents do a great job with big hearts and attention to detail. I think the purpose of the show is to demonstrate to viewers that you can have a big family and normal life.

I imagine that if I had eight children, I would go off the deep end. I look at families with multiple children as blessings, but just not my blessings. My God has given me the exact number that I can manage. One. Hmmm …. I think I'll go call one of my sisters now.

Adrian Jackson is a freelance writer in Beeville, Texas. She has a daughter, Abrianne; eight nephews -- Aaron, Troy, Travis, Alex, Michael, Harlem, Phoenix and Xavier; and five nieces – Heather, Desiree, Mo'neque, Rebekkah and Keyana.

A shy and awkward girl

I'm shy. I tell people this and they never believe me.

I was a shy kid. I was bony, gangly and almost always wore hand-me-downs. My hair was a fuzzy mess and I had (okay, have) a large forehead. I was self-conscious and awkward. I was neither a beautiful nor popular girl.

When I was in high school, I forced myself into situations where I'd have to speak up. I joined the cheerleading squad. I ran for homecoming queen (and won). I ran for student body vice-president (and lost). In this way, I gained confidence and learned to hide my shyness. By the time I graduated, I was well-known, well-liked and outspoken but still shy.

Today, I generally try to avoid social situations where I am required to be interesting or witty. I am a great talker, but only among those I am familiar with. I don't make friends easily. I'm no banterer or chatterbox. I'm the sort that gravitates towards someone I know and sticks with that one person all evening or I hover around the fringes hoping someone will strike up a conversation and invite me into it.

I'm terrible at small talk. I don't like to ask personal questions, so I don't. I answer questions effectively, but the discussion usually stays on me, since I am uncomfortable with the whole quid-pro-quo exchange. I don't know what to say and I don't want to ask inappropriate questions so I generally avoid social events where I may be forced into these situations.

Questions geared toward furthering a light discussion never enter my mind when I need them to. I never think to ask, "Did you hear about…?" or "Where are you from?" I just work off of the assumption that if they wanted me to know stuff they'd tell me.

I talk about myself a lot. It's not that I like to (though I am an interesting person). I just find it easier to answer questions than to ask them.

This is all contradictory to my career. I don't think I've ever had a job that didn't involve interaction with other people. As a reporter, I was always rooting around someone's mental basement. I've always been able to function in these instances. I can talk to an audience full of people but put me in a small group and I get terribly nervous. Worse still, put me at a dinner table with people I don't know well and I spend an inordinate amount of time staring at my plate.

Disney Movies

If you are a Disney Channel fan by proxy you know what High School Musical is. My daughter and billions of 'tweens the world over have gone mad for this made-for-TV movie and its poolside sequel. And, I have to admit, I've seen both and they are pretty good.

It is the sort of movie parents don't mind their kids watching. The sort of moms like me have come to expect from Disney. There's a positive message. There's teen romance (not like on the OC). There's singing, dancing and sports. There's beauty and brains.

Disney has taken this success to the bank. They've done what any capitalist mega-company would do – they took the show on the road. First, they released a music CD. Then they developed a stage play. There are also High School Musical and HSM2 dolls and toys.

And now, just in case you haven't had enough, Disney has announced an ice version of the movie. That's right, folks. High School Musical: The Ice Tour. How much is too much?

I think Disney banks on two facts – (1) 'tweens do not exhaust easily and (2) parents will pay for anything. Case and point is the mom who paid $1,000 for tickets to see Hannah Montana with her six year old. Will a six year old really appreciate a $1,000 concert? I doubt it. It's American overindulgence at its best and Disney is going to bet on the HSM horse until it collapses on the track.

They are going to take a perfectly good movie and squeeze the life out of it. They are going to overexpose this thing to the point of revulsion.

In Disney's defense, they've been very successful with this model in the past. Remember when the Lion King went to Broadway? It was so successful that most of Disney's animated movies followed in some form or another. Remember when the Cheetah Girls became a real singing group? They've been entertaining for years.

Finding Nemo On Ice is coming to Corpus Christi soon, just in case you didn't see the live play. We did and we loved it but I doubt we will check out the upcoming performance. Having a fish tale go from the ocean to land to ice is a bit too far in my opinion. Of course, Disney doesn't care what I think.

Least-loved child waits longest to be picked up

On the second day of school, thinking I had figured out when to show up so that I didn't sit in the pick-up lane at Thomas Jefferson Elementary School for an inordinate amount of time, I wound up at the back of the line – the very last car. As I navigated the road, the cones and the parking lot U, I realized, with dismay, that my daughter was the last one to be picked up. By the time I got to her the crossing guard has stored her stop sign and Coach Harvey had put the bullhorn down.

I was embarrassed and upset. Not because I am an overly dramatic person. It was because I've had one constant mantra since my daughter started school – The last child to be picked up is the least-loved child.

You can always spot the least-loved child. He sits on the curb hunched over, cradling his books in his arms with a forlorn look on his face. Her little head pops up every time a car goes by and sinks beneath her shoulder blades when she realizes that it's not *her* ride. This child is the one that school officials hover over with an exasperated look and a furiously tapping foot. Frequently, the least-loved child is the last to leave day after day after agonizing day.

All parents, on occasion, have struggled to get to the pick up lane on time and missed the mark. I have. But some never make it at the allotted time. Some parents are constantly late. Their lives outside of this single chore encroach on their ability to pick up their kid in a timely manner.

Why least loved? The child of those parents has to compete with unforeseen forces that pull the parent out of focus. The child of those parents is lower on the list of priorities than work or chores or shopping or phone calls. The child of those parents is but a single line item on a daily checklist of things to do. The child of those parents is not as important as other things in life.

I've always made a priority of picking up my daughter on time. No matter what I am doing, no matter where I am, I get to her school on time. I set an alarm at work to make sure that I am out the door at the right time, especially if she is out earlier than usual when I'm not in the mindset to pick her up in the middle of the day. Sometimes I carry a sticky note around with her name on it so that I don't lose track of time. Sometimes picking her up involves leaving in the middle of a meeting. Sometimes I have to cut off a conversation or walk out of my office early (and I am lucky enough to be able to do that). Sometimes I have to adjust my out-of-town schedule so that I'm back with enough time to make it to the school. I've cut it close a few times but the thought of her slumped over, anxiously waiting for my car to round the corner keeps me on my toes.

The emphasis on picking her up on time started in Pre-K and I've maintained it for years. I want her to know that she is so important to me that her school schedule is a part of my day. It is the least I can do to show her that I love her and I take her education seriously. It is a show of respect and yes, she notices.

On this particular occasion, I apologized profusely, explaining that I had misjudged the time that I expected to spend in line. She accepted my apology and said, 'Don't worry, Mom. There are lots of kids still here. The buses haven't left yet.' Thank goodness. She is not the least-loved child.

Don't give me a hand

One of the most troubling issues for me in business and social situations is the handshake.

I don't like the idea of touching the hands of people I don't know. To be honest, sometimes I don't like the idea of touching the hands of people I do know. I prefer not to shake hands at all.

I'm a frequent hand washer but I don't know to what degree other people are. It's not like you can look at someone and know right away that they don't wash their hands (okay, sometimes you can). It's not like there is a smell or color or mark or something. You just have to take your chances.

Handshaking is a daunting but necessary task. It is a part of our culture. Unlike taking off one's hat when entering a building or opening the door for a lady, it doesn't seem to be going out of style any time soon.

There is no way to avoid shaking hands without coming off blatantly rude. So I shake, but sometimes slip away to wash my hands shortly after.

And then there are the handshakes themselves. A handshake says a lot about a person and if you've got a bad one you should consider adopting a curt bow.

There is the weak shake – when the hand offered is droopy and almost lifeless. The connection is saggy and the message is: *I am without confidence. Please, take advantage of me.*

Another bad handshake is the crusher. It's the knuckle-squeezer that forces the receiving hand to crumble under pressure. It's aggressive and painful and frequently women are the victims most hurt by it. The message is: *I am strong. I will destroy your girly hand.*

There is also the shake that lasts too long. I don't know how long the exchange is supposed to last but I know when it has gone over the limit. The message is: *I have no concept of personal boundaries.*

Equally offending is the wet one. Eww. The giver's hand is clammy and moist. The receiver is left with more than a greeting. Call it a parting gift.

The hearty handshake is just fine on its own merits unless the up-and-down action is fast enough to pop your wrists. It is one of my favorite handshakes since the giver is usually a jovial person.

Another handshake I enjoy is the intimate handshake of women that I don't think men know about. It is almost like a sympathetic hand grab. It is a very feminine move. The message is: *We are sisters in spirit.*

I'm always concerned when I shake the hand of a person who suffers from arthritis. I think my firm, but not bone-crushing, handshake is too painful for someone who is already in pain. Would a weak handshake be more merciful? I don't know.

I like to shake hands with kids. I am always impressed when a youngster can give a crisp handshake. Show me a kid with a good handshake and I show you someone who was raised right.

I think my handshake stands up as well as anybody's. I haven't received any complaints thus far. If my handshake is not up to par, point that out to me. This is something I need to know.

Adrian Jackson is a freelance writer in Beeville, Texas. She is a little nuts about germs and keeps a bottle of antibacterial gel in her desk drawer, her purse and her car.

Who is a hero?

I recently saw an ad that said, "My Mom is a Weight Loss Hero!" It bugged me. The woman in the photo lost 130 pounds. That's respectable. Certainly worthy of praise. But a hero? I don't think so.

She didn't work off 130 pounds, which would be heroic. She went to a clinic and had a surgical weight loss procedure. She had every right in the world to do that and I'm not criticizing but is she a hero? Sure, if you call having your stomach cinched making it harder for you to digest the pounds and pounds of food that you shovel into your grill heroic. Call me a cynic but I don't think that is heroic at all.

There are soldiers out there fighting and dying for our country. Some fight long after their tour ends. Many face insurmountable odds. Others face situations that we lack the capacity to comprehend. Some return home bruised, battered and broken in spirit or limb and they are the lucky ones for having gotten out alive. They are heroes.

There are cancer survivors who struggle through cures that are frequently harder than the illnesses they address. They fight everyday for a chance at survival. They honor and support each other. They put on brave faces and pretend to be strong even when odds are not in their favor. They sacrifice their own well-being so that others can benefit from the knowledge gained. They subject themselves to stares, points and comments about bald heads, scars and moon faces and do so with grace and humor. They are heroes.

What about those who put the lives of others ahead of their personal safety and security? In the face of tragedy, large and small, we depend on our firemen, policemen, EMTs, doctors and nurses to get us out of harm's way. They are the one's moving forward when the rest of us are running away. They are heroes.

Teachers go to school every day. They teach our children the skills they need to achieve goals. They teach our kids to dare to dream about their personal futures. Teachers teach all of our children, regardless of who they are, what they look like, how smart they are, what language they speak. Teachers are heroes.

There are those in law enforcement who work hard to protect our families from harm. They are policemen, deputies, lawyers, judges and law makers who make our communities safe. They are heroes, too.

A woman who has a surgical weight loss procedure is not a hero. When we use the word in such a pedestrian manner, we diminish its true meaning.

Musicals are making a comeback

I found the soundtrack to "Oklahoma!" in a box. I suspect my daughter hid it years ago but I've got it now. It's not a contemporary music choice, I know, but musicals are back baby.

I've been a fan of musicals since I can remember. I grew up on the classics like "The King and I," "The Sound of Music" and "Cinderella." I've seen some shows live, at the movies and watched them on television.

I own a few soundtracks, but only just a few since the nerd meter goes up with every purchase, if you know what I mean.

I have a great love and appreciation for a good, solid musical. The combination of song, dance and delivery that transports you to another time and place is remarkable. The spectrum of emotions brought on and punctuated by song connects the viewer to the story in a way that happens in no other genre. Whether you are at a live performance or sitting in a dark living room, you can get caught up quickly. I'm sorry, but Arnold Schwarzenegger with a laser gun never made me feel the way Gene Kelly did when he sang *You Were Meant for Me*.

"Singin' in the Rain" is my all-time favorite but I've memorized "West Side Story" and "Mary Poppins" with equal enthusiasm. Another of my favorites is "Purlie." Melba Moore has an incredible vocal range and is accompanied by Robert Guillame (remember Benson?) and Sherman Hemsley (aka George Jefferson).

When I drove from Germany to Austria I popped in "The Sound of Music" and rolled down the windows. I sang at the top of my lungs as the snow-capped mountains came into view. Who can forget *Climb Ev'ry Mountain* or *Edelweiss*? Who didn't want to be 16 going on 17? Come on. Don't pretend that you don't know the words.

I took my daughter to a live performance of "Annie" earlier this year. "Annie" is a classic introduction to the theater for young girls. I was delighted that she absolutely loved it even though we had terrible seats. I don't know if it was because the actresses were all about her age or if the songs were just so lively but she really enjoyed herself. This thrilled me to no end. We are making plans to see "Wicked" when it comes to Texas next year and hope to squeeze in a few more shows between now and then.

Movie musicals lost their appeal at some point between the 1960s and 1980s. During the heyday of the 1950s, actors performed their songs on late night television so old performances of live productions are still around for us to enjoy. Julie Andrews as Eliza Doolittle singing *Wouldn't it be Loverly?* is a timeless clip.

Movie studios stopped putting up big bucks to produce movie musicals so for many years, those of us who really loved them had to stick with classics. New ones were few and far between. Of course there were some gems like "Rocky Horror Picture Show" and "Grease" and some stinkers like "Grease 2" (starring Michelle Pfeiffer) and "Hairspray" (starring Ricki Lake).

Today, with success of "Moulin Rouge," "Chicago" and "Rent" on screen, we are seeing a great resurgence of movie musicals. Disney deserves a great deal of credit for bringing up a new generation with movies like "High School Musical," of which the third installment will be released in theaters, not on television like the previous two. Gotta appreciate *Get'cha Head in the Game*.

The recently-released "Mama Mia," featuring ABBA's discography, is a gem. Who doesn't love the simplicity that is ABBA? The movie is a silly feminine romp on a Greek island but it is by far the best musical I've seen in a while. Can you listen to *Dancing Queen* without chiming in? I don't think so.

I'm glad for the resurgence of interest. I feel less like a geek and I look forward to seeing this movement grow and grow.

Death to the doppelganger

If I ever find the person who stole my identity, I'm gonna kill her. That may seem like a radical step, but once you get the gist of my story, you'll understand where I am, mentally.

Someone stole my identity in 1997. I don't know how she got it, but all of a sudden Adriane C. Jackson started working and paying taxes in North Carolina with my social security number. Naturally, Adriane C. Jackson has never held a job for very long and loves to buy things she can't afford. She's left a trail of utility bills, bank loans and an unpaid bill for $90 from Sampson County Airport in North Carolina. I've never even been to Sampson County!

What really aggravates me is that she is better at being me than I am. She is able to live successfully for more than a decade without ever facing the consequences of her actions. She files taxes almost every year and I think she always get hers in before mine. I have to wait until June before the Internal Revenue Service releases my return. The IRS is aware that there are two of us but doesn't seem to care enough to take any action. The IRS actually knew about the whole thing three years before I did but didn't make me aware or try to investigate the matter.

The Social Security Administration has also been aware of the two Adrians for years. I've tried several times to get them to investigate the matter, but they don't seem to care either. The alternate me has successfully changed the date of birth on my social security account, so apparently I got my first job at the age of seven.

If Adriane C. Jackson were a Nobel Prize-winning scientist or a movie star, I would gladly share my identity with her. If she had a steady paying job and paid her bills on time I wouldn't mind sharing at all. That would work out for both of us. But nooooooooo. She's just dragging me down. I pay 23 percent interest on my car loan. I doubt anybody will front me the mortgage on a house. I can't get instant credit or raise the spending limit on my Visa account. I'll never be asked to join a time-share vacation resort. When I try to explain the problem to creditors they give me the look. You know the look. It's the *stop-lying-you-just-have-bad-credit* look.

So, how do I get rid of this person? Death is really the only thing that will separate us. So, if I killed the person who stole my identity, who on paper is me, would it be considered suicide?

The other N word

I was in a meeting the other day and heard a woman refer to a group of people as negroes. The other N-word. I listened to her in stunned silence, doubting my own ears. *What? Did she just say Negroes? I'm sorry, have I stumbled into 1964?*

Now, in defense of people all over the country forced to keep up with what we are calling ourselves now this generation, I don't expect everyone to be up on *African-American*. I'm not even comfortable saying it. It is a mouthful. But this woman should have been able to come up with a better word. *Black* and *Afro-American* are outdated, but acceptable. *Colored* and *Negro* are not. There is another word but I strongly discourage anyone from using it, even though some of us may give you the impression that we use it amongst ourselves quite frequently. We don't.

I wasn't angry with this woman but I was upset. Being the only black person in the room, I was also uncomfortable.

It is difficult to imagine that an educated woman in the 21st century has lived such a sheltered life that she didn't realize that the term is offensive. In a rural Texas county where African-Americans represent less than 11 percent of the population, it's possible that she has had little contact with *us*. Maybe her terminology never evolved past the 1960s. But both seem unlikely to me. So what gives? Does she routinely refer to African-Americans as Negroes? And, has she managed to get this far in life without being corrected or does she not care to be politically correct? If the answer to both questions is yes, then have I over-reacted? Or, have I under-reacted?

I hate political correctness. Who can keep up with the ethnic, physical, gender preferential boxes that we like to cram ourselves into? Who cares about how we puff ourselves up with verbose classifications? On the other hand, we have to be sensitive to others. We are, in fact, a diverse culture. We are special that way.

How can we be more sensitive or less offensive? We could ignore the color of people's skin. But you can't. The thing about skin color is you can see it a mile away. It's the first attribute you see on a person. Anybody who says they don't see skin color is either blind or not telling the truth. Of course you see it. It's right there. The trick is to not let the color of someone's skin be an indication of their character. The color of skins unifies us but it doesn't define who we are. If we can remember that and live by it, we can get somewhere together.

Sept 11: Am I ready to be entertained?

A movie about Sept. 11 is now in theaters. It makes me wonder if we are ready for a movie about one of the biggest tragedies of our times. Or, a bigger question, am I?

I was born and raised in New Jersey. I could see the Twin Towers from a bridge near my grandmother's house. When I was little we used to walk to that bridge with lawn chairs and watch the fireworks over New York City. It was our July 4th tradition.

I've been to the World Trade Center many times. The Twin Towers were elegant but imposing. They were goddesses and sentinels. They could be seen from everywhere. Sometimes, when they swayed, if you were inside you could feel it. I've been inside but never went to the top of the towers because I thought it was a goofy tourist thing to do. Now, I regret that.

I've been to the Twin Towers site since Sept. 11, 2001. I took my daughter in 2005. We stood behind a fence staring into a gaping scar in the Earth. It was surreal and very sad. It was like a trip to Dachau. You could feel the loss of human life and despair permeating the atmosphere. If you've ever been to a place like that, you understand what I mean. If you've never been, you are missing out on one of the great human emotional experiences.

I'm glad I went to the World Trade Center because I think it's an obligation of the survivors to preserve the memory of those who lost their lives. And, we are all survivors regardless of where we were when those towers came down. We are the ones who will tell the stories to our children and grandchildren. We are the writers of history. We have a moral responsibility to get the story right. And, to make it memorable.

We take the easy route by turning that responsibility over to Hollywood but we can't let Hollywood take over the telling of the story. We have to be vigilant and ensure that the seriousness of the story is not compromised.

But it's that seriousness that I'm afraid of. I've got a personal connection with those towers. I don't know if I can remain emotionally detached enough to enjoy the movie but I feel like I have to watch it.

Am I ready for this?

I like to cry at movies. I think if you don't leave the theater with the sniffles, it wasn't worth the two hours you spent watching it. But the crying comes from getting caught up in a fantasy. At the end, it is for entertainment purposes only. I remain detached and my emotional reaction is always a superficial one.

Even movies like "Schindler's List" and "Pearl Harbor," based on actual events, had enough of a movie quality to them that I could remove myself from the reality and enjoy the movie. If you've ever seen "Schindler's List" it is an emotionally exhausting movie. But since it is a 60-year old story, I don't have a real connection to it. Not so with the World Trade Center.

Can I detach myself enough to be entertained?

This is not the first movie. There've been television movies. Recently, one movie won an Emmy award. I missed that movie. I missed them all. I didn't want to see them. But I don't think I should avoid the subject any longer. I'm going to see this one. What about you?

Olympic hopeless gears up for summer games

After 37 years of demonstrating absolutely no aptitude or natural ability for any sort of sport or athletic contest, I thought I could safely give up my dream of competing in the Olympics. And then came Dara Torres, the 40-year old wunderkind of the swim world. Torres is out there proving that 40-year-olds can do anything. Wow.

While the young, fresh-faced athletes get most of the attention and resemble our ideal of an Olympic athlete, there are many competitors in Torres' peer group. Libby Callahan of South Carolina is ranked the top U.S. competitor in Women's Pistol Shooting. She's 56. Richard "Butch" Johnson, a 52-year-old from Connecticut, is an archer. This is his fifth trip to the Olympics. Equestrian Beezie Madden is 45.

Bowler Patrick Allan is almost 38. Heather Corrie, who will represent the U.S. Canoe/Kayak team in the whitewater slalom, recently celebrated her 37th birthday. Lisa Leslie, a basketballer, is a 36-year-old. Cyclist George Hincapie of South Carolina was born in 1973. This is his fifth trip to the big show and he's got ten Tour de Frances under his spokes. Brian Olson, a 35-year-old Tallahassee native, made the U.S. Judo Team.

We 30- to 40-year olds are well represented at this summer's games. I am proud of my compatriots and I'm looking forward to seeing them take to the field, floor, road, pool, track and course.

As hard as Torres and all of our American athletes have worked to obtain the honor of representing our country in Beijing, isn't there a little Olympic spirit in all of us? Haven't we all thought, 'Sure, I'll never win a medal in gymnastics but I can shoot at least as good as Geena Davis (who ranked high in her sport but did not make the U.S. archery team a decade ago).'

I love the Olympics because it is where dreams come true. I never dreamed of taking part in the summer Olympics. I was never a fast runner. A mile in the pool is counted in hours for me. And I couldn't hit the red side of a barn with a water balloon, let alone a precision weapon of any kind.

I always dreamed of being a figure skater. Yes, unoriginal, I know. But there is something magical about skating that captures the imagination. It is the sport equivalent of being a princess and what little girl doesn't want to be a princess?

As far as athleticism, I was never actually very good at skating. Though I love it to this day and still ice skate when the chance presents itself, my skills are limited to not falling down and being able to go fast (not fast enough for speed skating).

So, though I'm still young enough to compete in the Olympics, I doubt I'll ever make the U.S. team. I'm what you might call an Olympic hopeless. But I'll watch the dreams of athletes like Torres come true. I'll hoot and holler with every American victory this summer.

Good luck to all of the athletes representing our country in Beijing. Go USA!

The Oscar goes to...

When a movie wins an Oscar, I feel I have to run out and see it right away. My logic is if it won such a prestigious award – especially in one of the top categories -- it must certainly be an excellent movie. This, unfortunately, is not always the case.

The award for the stupidest movie ever to win an Oscar for Best Picture goes to ... "The English Patient" (1996). This drivel won nine Oscars. The story of a burned WWII pilot and a nurse, who appear to be two of the last four people on Earth, drags on and on with a series of staccato flashbacks that do little more than break up the monotony of the main story. I didn't *get* this movie. I didn't enjoy it. I want my three hours back.

The award for the franchise that will not go away goes to ... "Rocky." Because of movies about a washed-out Philly boxer with a speech impediment I've been teased my whole life. That's right. Rocky's wife's name was Adrian. Actually, it was A-D-R-I-A-N!!!!!! This 1976 Best Pic winner has spawned yet another sequel and for that it deserves to die.

The award for creepiest actor in a movie with inappropriate subject matter goes to .... Kevin Spacey. If lusting after your teenage daughter's tarty friend earns you an Oscar, then Spacey deserved the one he got in 1999 for "American Beauty." Movies about the sexuality of young girls upset me, but I didn't vote.

The award for actor most likely to be cast as loser/boozer goes to ... Nicholas Cage. "Leaving Las Vegas" earned Cage an Oscar in 1995. The movie about a man, a prostitute and a lot of liquor left me unimpressed. I'm a huge fan of Cage, but this movie, like "The English Patient," seemed to drag on forever. He went to Vegas to die and I was rooting for him.

The award for pretty actress able to morph into psycho goes to ... Charlize Theron. She won an Oscar in 2003 for her portrayal of a serial killer in "Monster." I wanted to like this movie, but how could I when the main character was so unlovable? This movie was tedious, weird and shot from bizarre camera angles.

The award for high concept movie that totally went over my head goes to .... "The Hours." I actually watched "The Hours" twice. This movie earned Nicole Kidman an Oscar in 2002. After reading the book, *Mrs. Dalloway*, for an English class, I was advised to watch the film again. I didn't like it the first time or the second time. I got the connection, I just didn't care. And don't get me started on Kidman, one of my least favorite actresses. I am still angry with her about "Dead Calm."

The award for most unfunny animated film series known to man goes to … "Wallace & Gromit in The Curse of the Were-Rabbit." There are people in this world who find Wallace and Gromit amusing. Those are the ones who awarded the movie an Oscar in 2005. I am not one of those people. Watching Wallace and Gromit is for me like sitting through a piano recital filled with first-year students. Enough said.

Smell my pits, you freak!

Have you heard of the new scented deodorants? As if Shower Fresh, Powder Scented and Lavender weren't enough, now there's Artic Apple, Vanilla Chai and Brazilian Cherry. It's like a dessert under there. What will they think of next?

When it comes to deodorant, I'm a traditionalist. I'm also very sensitive. I go with Unscented. My deodorant has to be without scent (because sometimes even Unscented has a fragrance). When I can't find my regular brand, I pop open containers at the store and sniff them to make sure that there is no smell emanating from them. I can't stand the smell of perfume or fruit under my arms.

Sugar-sweet pits drive me mad. I don't want to smell like morning dew or watermelon or blackberry pie. I want to smell like nothing. I am very selective about the deodorant I buy to achieve that smell.

Where are the wackos that like to smell armpits, anyway? *Oh, dear, is that Kuku Coco Butter deodorant you are wearing? Yes? I thought so. It smells lovely.* Ick! What kind of freak is going to appreciate your pit scent?

I recently read an article about how deodorant companies are trying to give consumers the option of matching scents with moods or outfits. Give me a break! Can spare 10 minutes in the morning to decide which smell best suits your level of optimism for the day? What if you put on peach-scented antiperspirant and got fired? Can you blame in on the deodorant or is your life just the pits?

I lived in Europe for more than a decade. Up until recently, few Europeans wore antiperspirant. Most of what you could buy were perfumed sprays that were designed to cover up one's natural smell, not diminish perspiration. And let me tell you, it was like stuffing roses in your hiking boots. Sure you can smell the roses, but that ain't the only scent coming out of there.

I think deodorant manufacturers are trying to compete with perfume manufacturers. But if I want to smell like perfume, I use perfume. I want my deodorant manufacturer to keep his eyes on the prize. Make a deodorant that doesn't stain, reduces sweat and keeps my pits from smelling. That's really all I need.

If you like the idea of underarm scents, raise your hand. On second thought, put your arm down.

Hollywood is beckoning me

This is my shot at the big time. The Writers Guild of America union members have gone on strike and this is my chance to move to Hollywood. For anyone who has ever turned on the TV and thought, 'I could do that,' here is our big chance.

Remember the last writers' strike? It killed the top-rated show 'Moonlighting' with Bruce Willis and Cybill Shepherd. The replacement writers took the show to the point of no return and when the original writers returned after almost half a year there was nothing left to salvage. Not even viewers. Of course, the downfall of the show worked out okay for the actors in the end.

But what about my dreams? I was just a teenager during the last writers' strike. Not old enough to light out across country. But I'm an adult now.

I could write for ER. Frankly, they need me over there. The writing has stunk for about four years now. I don't watch it anymore.

I started watching that show from the beginning. I can recall every character and every situation. I remember the pilot. I remember when Dr. Ross was a womanizer and when Dr. Benton found out that his son wasn't his son. I bawled my eyes out when Dr. Green died. I saw the irony when Dr. Romano was killed by a helicopter. But it was then that I realized that the last of the good writers had left the building.

I could certainly see myself writing for Grey's Anatomy. I've got the talent to write for that show. Seriously. First of all, I love that show. I know all the characters. Many are about my age, so I've got a point of reference. I can relate to what's going on. I could master the lingo. I could put a stop to the Izzie/George in love storyline before it does the show in. I could so be a writer on that show.

The one bad thing about taking advantage of this strike to further my own writing career is that I'd be a scab. I'd be a strike-breaker. The real writers would throw things at me as I entered the building to pursue my dreams. I'd have to bust through union lines. My grandfather, a longtime Teamster, would turn over in his grave. My mother, a die-hard liberal, would be ashamed and disappointed.

Another negative is that I support the writers' on getting their fair share of internet profits derived from their creative work. This means that I'll have to strike in solidarity. I will defer my dream of being a television drama writer and stand shoulder-to-shoulder with my brethren. I'm not going to write another column until next week.

Shopping cart rules

Who wrote the rules on shopping cart etiquette?

When my daughter was a baby, I almost never returned my cart to the parking stand. If you've ever shopped with an infant, you know that there is nowhere to stash the baby while you are pushing a cart a mile away to the nearest parking stand. You try to park next to a cart park but this is not always possible. Sure, you could push the baby to the parking stand and carry him back but is this really an option? I never thought so.

Now that my daughter is almost ten, one of us parks the cart. She thinks it's fun. But if the parking stand is more than ten cars away, there is no way I'm going to either go that far away or allow my kid to. Walking long distances with a shopping cart is dangerous.

In this instance, I push my cart to the nearest light post, striped area or store entrance. Is this acceptable? It seems that as long as I haven't taken up any parking spaces or put it in a place where it can roll into someone's vehicle, it's okay. Am I wrong?

In some parts of Europe, you have to pay to *rent* the cart. It makes for honest people. If shoppers don't return their carts they risk losing as much as $2. People buy plastic coins and keep them handy to use at the grocery store. Of course, these are the same people who bring their own shopping bags.

They tried cart rental in Killeen, Texas. I guess they figured that many service members and their families were used to this, having lived in Europe. It failed. Some people thought that once they paid to use the cart it became theirs so they pushed them home. Needless to say, that ended the practice. Americans are just not ready to have to pay for carts. Though, I've noticed that parents are willing to pay for those toddler carts that play music. If paying to hear the Wiggles will keep a child quiet and distracted while I am trying to shop, I'll pay for it. I wish they had one for nine-year-olds.

Nowadays, you can put a cover over the cart so that your baby isn't contaminated. I love this thing. Too bad they didn't have it when my daughter was a baby. If you've never taken a baby shopping, here's a startling fact: Babies like to suck on the cart bar. It is probably safer to let a kid play with toilet water than to allow her to put this horrible thing in her mouth. And there aren't enough hand wipes in the world to protect your child against the germs living on that nasty thing.

So somebody invented a plastic barrier, attached a toy and probably made millions. Parents spread these things over the cart seat and plunk the baby into them – instant germ control. I love it!

And while on the subject of carts, can I just say that using a cart doesn't immediately entitle the driver to take up the entire grocery aisle by stopping it in the middle. We all have carts and we are all trying to shop so how about a little courtesy? How about pulling over and letting others pass? The aisles are barely large enough for two-way traffic so a little cart etiquette goes a long, long way.

Teen pregnancy is not cool

It doesn't matter if there was a pact or not, teenage pregnancy is never a good idea. And while adults in Gloucester, Mass. scramble to assign blame we can rest assured that there is plenty to go around. What is the matter with parents and society when a gang of high school girls thinks it would be fun to get knocked up together?

Parents like me feel most secure in the knowledge that it is someone else's kid *in trouble*, not ours. The truth of it is that sometimes the fact that our daughters are not pregnant has more to do with pure coincidence than abstinence or sensibility.

Teenagers, boys and girls, are exposed to sexuality at very young ages. They get information from television (biggest offender), magazines, friends and adults. While most kids won't be confronted with blatant sexuality until they are in high school, early subliminal signs impact their opinions and actions later in life.

I have a friend who brings a new live-in boyfriend home about once a year. While her kids may not be aware of the sexual nature of the couple they are certainly learning about relationships, love and the transitory characteristics of men. Sure, I know that this is an altered version of reality but what do you think the ten-year-old daughter thinks about men? How do you think the 12-year-old son will treat women?

We like to blame the media for its sexual content but when we fail to be filters we are just as culpable. We get lulled into safety zones like Disney Channel and Nickelodeon and forget to do our jobs. Just when we think it's safe to loosen the reins a little Jamie Lynn Spears pops up pregnant and we have to explain that to our little girls. On the other hand, who would have ever thought that Miley Cyrus would appear nearly nude in a national magazine? I didn't see that one coming.

As a society, we hear so much about sexuality that we are no longer shocked or offended. Sexual perversion, whether criminal or preferred, is discussed with the commonality of dress patterns. People have come to feel the need to share their sexual lives in vivid detail at work, on television and on their cell phones. Sex talk is no longer left to late, late night cable networks. Our kids get the impression that sex is no longer intimate or sacred.

I don't think sex is a bad thing. Sex is a beautiful thing. I just think it should remain taboo. The transition from innocent to sexually-active is no longer a marked event, but an unremarkable next step in a process that happens all too publically.

Pregnancy, according to the media, is *en vogue*. It's chic. It's cool. It's the *baby bump*. Hollywood will have you believe that having a baby is like getting one of those hand-held Chihuahuas – an accessory. The reality for teenagers like the Gloucester Girls is that a baby is nothing but hardship. Someone said the only thing worse than a 17-year-old having a baby is a baby having a 17-year-old mom.

High schoolers are by nature narcissistic and unfocused. That's okay. That is what we expect from teenagers. But can a parent afford to be that way? And what about the socio-economic problems of teenage pregnancy? What about the absence of skills or the lack of a sustainable income? What about the statistical likelihood of disaster? Who foots the bill for unwed, unattached parents who are not employable and didn't finish high school? While not every teen parent turns out to be a statistic, we are supporting millions of them.

My sister was an unwed teenage mother. By the time she was 20 she was married to a ne'er-do-well with three kids and one on the way. The odds were stacked against her and she struggled for decades, losing custody of two of her children along the way. Today she is the mother of seven; three college-educated adults, three high school students, and one unwed mother. Her story is one of success, but it is uncommon.

For me and my two other sisters, it was my oldest sister's example that kept us from having sex. We grew up hearing 'don't be like your sister' and looking at her struggles I knew that hers was not the life for me.

But for the teens in Gloucester the damage is already done. The road ahead is paved with calamity. Babies are a blessing but in these cases it is unlikely that any of the tiny victims of this debacle will live a fortunate life.

Word

Ginormous. It's a word. It's official.

Merriam Webster recently announced that ginormous and 99 other words have been incorporated into its lexicon. I've used ginormous for years. It's a great word and I don't know why it's taken this long for the rest of the country to get on board. It's an amalgamation of gigantic and enormous. According to Merriam Webster, it's been around since 1948. There is a process that words go through before they can be accepted into common language. It's called neologism. Who knew?

Words are first introduced and used in small groups. As time goes on, they gain a wider audience of acceptance. Lastly, words gain widespread recognition. At this point they usually become part of our dictionaries. Many words come from scientific, technical, military or political communities. **IED** was added to the list this year. It is the abbreviation of "improvised explosive device." **Islamofascists** was also added this year.

Some words come from the hip hop community. Badonkadonk didn't make the list, but it is on the rise. Maybe next year? **Crunk** made the list. It is a Southern style of rap music or a form of hip hop dance that involves rapid, violent movements. So, if you want to get crunk, you just go right ahead. It's allowed.

Some words come out of pop culture. This year, **smackdown** debuts. If you don't know what a smackdown is, you need only go as far as professional wrestling. **Bollywood**, the call name for the movie industry in India also made the list. **Telenovela**, a Spanish word for serial or soap opera, has been added to our language.

Foodies (already in the dictionary) will be happy to know that **microgreens** made this year's list. Microgreens are small salad shoots.

DVR, digital video recorder, was also added this year. **Sudoku**, a 9x9 grid number puzzle, made its debut. The source of this word is Japan, where the game became highly popularized. Speed dating is now a part of our lexicon.

In 2006, words added to the dictionary included **ringtone**, **biodiesel**, **gastric bypass** and **super size**. **Sandwich generation**, **drama queen**, **polyamory** and **spyware** also made it to the list.

I'm hoping that bigonical (big and mechanical), booyah (an expression of glee) and bondiggidy (great) makes it to next year's list. I'm going to launch a campaign. Are you with me?

New Words

Merriam-Webster recently released its 2007 Words of the Year and all I can say is huh? On the top of the list is **w00t**. I don't know this word. I don't even know how to pronounce it. It is an interjection, according to Merriam-Webster Dictionary. It is derived from the truncation of words as a result of text messaging.

I think that if the word does not transcend from written language to speech, it shouldn't qualify. But apparently the majority of voters disagree.

I like a word I can roll around in my mouth for a while. I like one that makes a quirky sound like snarky, ginormous or tempestuous. Those are words I can use. I'm a little disappointed with this year's words. Most are uninspiring.

Facebook made the list. That's a faddish word. It means to look someone up on a social website. Example: I *facebooked* my new friend to see if he was legit.

Conundrum (a quizzical problem), **quixotic** (foolishly impractical), **hypocrite** (a person who puts up a front to mask his true beliefs), **apathetic** (unfeeling) and **charlatan** (a fake) made the list. These are old words with solid etymologies. They must all be *en vogue* again.

Blamestorm is a new word. It is a meeting held to assign responsibility for a failed project, according to the dictionary.

Pecksniffian made the list. Its roots are Dickensian. It means hypocritically self-righteous. I try to stay away from words derived from names. Machiavellian, Shakespearean and Bushies. If a reader doesn't know the history of the word, the meaning is completely lost.

Sardoodledom is the most unusual word to make the list this year. It is a noun, synonymous to melodrama. It is both an old word and a derivative of a name.

Words from the previous year were much better. They included truthiness, coined by Stephen Colbert of Comedy Central's The Colbert Report. Google, terrorism and insurgent also made the list. Those are all good, relevant, usable words. Decider, made popular by President George W. Bush, made the 2006 list too.

Merriam-Webster Online has a website for kids to submit made-up words and their definitions. Words from this list follow:

Blabachatter: to talk too much was submitted by Roxyana of California.

Alex from Illinois submitted crackatackle which means sweet and crunchy to eat.

A sweetaholic is a person who loves to eat sweets, according to Tasha of the United Kingdom.

Someone in South Korea submitted jokenik, which is a person who tells funny jokes.

Some of these words should have made the list.

I am a big fan of great words and believes that our traditional language is being strangled by dumb words like w00t.

Environment on the minds of dictionary makers

My favorite trendy word is **staycation**. It's a vacation that you spend at home, according to Merriam-Webster Online who just released their New Words of 2009.

Other trendy words to make it to the dictionary this year are **acai** (that South American weight-loss berry); **frenemy** (someone who pretends to be your BFF but actually is a big, fat backstabber); and **webisode** (a television show via the internet). These are good inclusions though a couple are way overused and on the verge of just being annoying.

Speaking of annoying, 'green speak' is infiltrating our language as well. **Green-collar**, like blue-collar but related to the environment, is in. **Locavore** looks like a Latinate word but is really a derivative of local and herbivore meaning someone who buys and consumes locally grown produce. It is a good word in the sense that it captures a positive movement but bad in that it seems fussy and overly complicated. It's the kind of word that makes you sound pretentious and makes others ask you to repeat and explain. **Carbon footprint**, the negative impact that something or someone leaves on the planet, made the list too.

Lots of medical and scientific words were included this year. Memory foam, that polyurethane stuff that molds to whatever it is pressed against, made it. **Cardioprotective** (anything that serves to protect the heart); **neuroprotective** (anything that serves to protect neurons); **naproxen** (a generic drug that diminishes pain and fever); **pharmacogenetics** (the study of patient response to drugs based on genetics); and **physiatry** (physical and rehabilitative medicine) were also added.

Words that have seeped into our language from the government and military made the list. **Earmark** (the allocation or to allocate funds for special projects); and **waterboarding** (a form of torture that simulates drowning) are now part of the dictionary.

Zip line, that cord that holds a harness that allows a person to slide (or zip) from one location to another, is on the list but it seems to me that it should have been included years ago because it is not really a new phrase. Did the Merriam-Webster judges miss the 1993 Stallone movie where the girl falls to her death after the zip line snaps over a cliff?

Vlog made the list. It is a video-based blog. I like the word 'blog' because it introduced us to something completely new but vlog takes it a too far. I don't think we have to modify every single word in the dictionary to make it sound internet savvy. It's like adding a lower case i to stuff — iSpot, iCam, iZine, iPhone, iTunes — we get it, we get it, enough already.

Sock puppet is on the 2009 list. It has a new, sinister definition. While the previous mention may have brought to mind fuzzy hand animals like a certain lovable and slightly edgy monkey, it now means a person on the internet with a fake identity used for malevolent purposes.

I'd like to see adorkable make the 2010 list. It describes a boy who is both cute and nerdy. Words I'd like to see taken out of the dictionary are bling-bling (haven't we used it enough?) and utilization (just say use).

The thrill is gone

I was 12. My name was Jackson. I had a plastic jacket just like his. My sister's room was covered in Jackson posters torn out of Tiger Beat magazine. Yes, it was the 1980s and if you didn't live it, you don't get it. Am I right?

When we got cable and could watch music videos, we were the coolest kids around. We liked MTV. We watched music videos as much as we could. MTV was all videos, so if the television was on, that is what was playing. We knew all the songs and all the stars. We could sing anything by Madonna, David Bowie or The Eurythmics, word-for-word.

We knew who Michael Jackson was. We had grown up on the Jackson 5. We'd watched them on television, bought their records and saw the cartoons. (Yes, there were cartoons.) We owned "Off the Wall," Jackson's coming out album.

And then, there was "Thriller." Song after song was a huge hit. Jackson sang *The Girl is Mine* with Paul McCartney (He was a big star from my mom's generation). There were other collaborations with names like James Ingram and Eddie Van Halen. Quincy Jones produced the album.

There was *Beat It* and *Billie Jean*, both mega-hits with stupendous videos. Jackson started the group dancing that is so prevalent in today's music videos. The choreography in *Beat It* is out of this world. The light show in *Billie Jean* seems silly now but was a techno-wonder in the 1980s.

Thriller was off the charts. As if the song wasn't awesome enough, the video was released. It changed the face of videos. *Thriller* actually validated the work of videographers and video directors. *Thriller* expanded the perimeters of what could be done in a video. Jackson also brought big names into the new genre. John Landis directed the video. Landis rose to fame for "Animal House," "The Blues Brothers," "American Werewolf in London," "Trading Places" and "Coming to America." Vincent Price had a voiceover on the album and a role in the video, which was more like a featurette.

We saw the very first MTV airing of the video. It had been publicized, so we were ready when it came. But really, we weren't ready at all. No one was. *No one.* This video broke the mold and blew our minds. We had never seen anything like it. It was a little scary, a little intriguing and way cool. It was epic. We all walked away a little different.

Fast forward 25 years...

I'm not 12 anymore. I am a mother and Michael Jackson is, well, creepy, weird and scary-looking. I cannot support his music. Jackson is rare in that he has so completely eradicated the person he was. The difference is really black and white.

"Thriller" and "Off the Wall" were made by the cute black kid from the Jackson 5. I can still listen to the old stuff and enjoy it because I can disassociate him from the bony white guy who likes to cup himself. But enjoying music and padding Jackson's coffers with proceeds from CD sales are not the same. I won't buy the special release CD. The thrill is gone.

Oh, how I love bacon

There is a cafeteria where I work. At about 10:30 some mornings, the smell of the grills waif up the hill to the building I work in. And can I say *it is marvelous*?! Any day I am halted by the smell of frying bacon is a good day for me.

As much as I adore bacon, I realize that I can't eat it every day. Or even every week. But there are no calories in the smell.

A friend of mine recently turned me on to turkey bacon. I was skeptical. Turkey is a healthier choice (though, honestly, I don't know what preservatives and flavors they put into it) but you have to be willing to give up something. I'd tried ground turkey (ick!) and turkey sausage (ugh!) and couldn't make the switch. I didn't find them at all appealing and it amazes me that there is a market for some of these products. But, back to bacon. I enjoyed the turkey bacon. It was crispy, crunchy and fried. What more could I want?

Now, I will admit that turkey bacon is not like the honey smoked pork bacon laced with the perfect combination of fat and meat. It is this delicate balance that makes bacon the wonderful thing that it is. I would never eat a pork chop with that much fat on it. I actually gave up pork chops years ago.

Could I give up bacon? Probably not. Oh, I've tried but I find that there are some things I'm not willing to live without. Like French fries. I've tried to give up fries but they are my weakness. Those perfect little, rectangular, deep fried, golden brown treats. How could I ever reject that kind of goodness?

While I would never eat an imitation French fry, I would consider switching my bacon. And to ease the transition, I've discovered Bacon Salt. Can there actually be a salt that takes like bacon? Really? I have to admit that I've never actually tasted it but I've heard rave reviews.

I didn't grow up eating salt. My mother had some strict rules about salt and I never cared for the taste. I got through my first 36 years of life with little salt in my diet until I discovered salt grinders. Big rocks of salt are whittled down to manageable crystals that cling to corn and fries like little daggers. The taste of real salt is so much better than that powdery crap.

And now they've added bacon? Bacon Salt is fat free and has zero calories. If that is not enough, it is also Kosher. What more do you want?

Forget Paris Hilton

I think we can all rest easy in the knowledge that Paris Hilton is home from prison. I know I feel better knowing that after 20 very, very long days, our Paris is back on this side of those iron bars. And having obviously read Martha Stewart's book, 'Prison for Dummies,' Paris was released with all the flash and fanfare appropriate of someone of her status. And, she gracefully remembered to thank the losers ... er, I mean, little people.

What I want to know is why? Not why did this happen to Paris. Why do I have to hear about it? No matter where you go you've no doubt come across this story. Television media hasn't put this much coverage on a single story since OJ tried on the glove. Yeesh!

I haven't kept up with Paris' story. It is only through osmosis that I've been able to absorb the gist. I'm no Paris Watcher. I didn't watch her television show. I don't keep up with her in the tabloids. Yet, I know more than anyone really needs to know about the celeb.

Unless you've spent the last month under a rock, you've seen and heard about Paris at least once every hour. What she did in prison. What she ate in prison. What she wore in prison. What she said in prison. You get the idea.

It drives me crazy that there is so much media attention on Paris, when there are many more important stories to cover. With the exception of the two women who stood outside the prison holding FREE PARIS signs, I haven't come across a single person who is fervently following this story. Newscasters say they are following the story because its what their viewers want to know about, but I don't know anybody eager to stay abreast of new developments.

I think this is indicative of our current news culture. The lines between real news and real junk is blurred. You used to find stories like this one on entertainment news shows where they belonged. Now they come out as the lead on the 6 o'clock news and everybody's clamoring to get the biggest scoop.

You can't rely on any single network to give you just news. You can't even rely on networks that are devoted to news. One network interrupted a political interview to cover Paris getting in a car.

I get most of my news from The Daily Show with John Stewart. I find it refreshing and thought provoking. What does it say about us when our fake news is better at presenting news than real news?

I hate homework

Parents, if my daughter is in tears by the time her homework is done, am I doing something wrong?

This is our scenario:

We get home with about three hours left to eat, do homework and shower. Needless to say we are moving pretty fast at this point.

My daughter usually has a portion of her homework already completed. So we split into teams -- the doer and the checker. I've found that sitting together during this period is difficult. I can't watch the way she does her homework because it is a disorganized nightmare of falling pages, flying erasers and using toes to rub the cat. It drives me crazy but it doesn't seem to bother her at all unless I'm standing over her shrieking about the importance of focusing on the task at hand. So, the checker, me, has to leave the room.

Invariably she will come upon a question she doesn't know the answer to. The answer seems pretty simple to me, but of course, I've already passed the third grade. I try to explain the answer in a way that leads her to it without giving it away but since her learning style is different than my teaching style we stumble over it for about ten minutes when it probably would have taken her teacher two minutes to explain. Voices are raised. Arms are flailed. She thinks that I think that she is stupid and I think that she thinks I'm stupid.

I have to sign her homework. I won't sign it unless I've looked at it. *Unreasonable policy, I know.* She shows me her work in her typical disorganized fashion and I have to refer to her planner to figure out what exactly the assignment is before I can assess whether or not it has been completed. I have to decipher my daughter's handwriting which is as bad as mine. I have to read stories in order to check the answers. I have to work the math to check the answers. They use new techniques in math not the ones popular in the last century.

If I find an error I call my daughter to correct it. This upsets her and I'm not sure why. Is she upset that it is not perfect? Is she upset because I called her on it? I have no idea.

After the homework is done, we go through graded work in her folder. If she has a high number of wrong answers on her paper we discuss it. I ask, 'did you not understand the assignment? Were you paying attention? Did you read the instructions? Did you ask for help?'

These seem like acceptable questions but the response I get is usually a bout of tears or eye-rolling. My daughter, like her mother, is an over achiever. I suspect admitting to her teacher that she doesn't understand something is like admitting failure in her mind. When I suggest writing the teacher a note asking her to explain the assignment again, my daughter goes ballistic.

Is this typical behavior or am I doing something wrong?

Will I ever succeed in math?

I took five years of math during my four years in high school (Algebra I, Algebra II, Geometry, Trig and Pre-Calc). So, it comes as no surprise that I signed up for Calculus when I arrived at Seton Hall University. I thought I could handle it but I was mistaken. I failed. My first and second attempts. Okay, I got a 'D' the second time around but college Ds are not transferable.

A decade later, returning to college, I was demoted. I was placed in high school Algebra I and had to crawl back up to College Algebra. I struggled but with great perseverance I prevailed and passed and graduated. When it was all over, I thought to myself, gleefully, 'I never have to take another math class in my life!'

Well, I was mistaken. Here I am in fourth grade math – again.

First, second and third grade math were a breeze. My daughter's math homework went something like – addition, subtraction, addition, subtraction, fractions, addition, subtraction, multiplication, addition, subtraction. Pretty easy stuff. Even for me. And then we got to the fourth grade, I expected it to be challenging but already I'm in over my head. We are studying division (okay, I can handle that), estimation (that's fairly easy) and theory (whoa, are you kidding me?!).

When my daughter asked what a divisor was, I could only respond, 'I dunno.' I am so far past the basics that I don't remember them anymore. What I do remember had different names back in the 1970s. They also get to the answers by a different route nowadays. Trying to discuss a problem is like trying to have a conversation with someone who doesn't speak the same language. There are a lot of grunts and hand gestures and we both walk away frustrated.

I don't get the class lecture or the practice assignments leading up to the homework. Since I'm not sitting in my daughter's class when the work is discussed, I rely on memory, skill and a bachelor's degree in History. If you give me a word problem on the spot I'll freeze and maybe burst into tears.

I have to fly blind to check my daughter's worksheet. The only way to check the work is to actually do, so I do.

One math question recently stumped both of us. We spent a lot of time discussing it and neither could figure out how to solve it. It was a word problem. Word problems were never my strong suit but my daughter usually has a knack for them. This one was a riddle, too. *Oh, joy!* See if you can find the answer:

Maci is playing a game with her brother Ty. She said she would pick a number and give clues to its identity. Also, for every number Ty guessed right, she would do two sit-ups. The clues she gave are (#1) The number is an odd number; (#2) The sum of the digits is 5 and (#3) The number is less than 25. What number did Ty guess? How many sit-ups will Maci have to do?

My daughter skipped the first question and incorrectly answered 2 on the second question. My answer? 'I dunno.'

I often tell people that I'm a writer so I shouldn't have to be responsible for math. I've never had a head for it to the great disappointment of my algebra teacher Mr. John Tonero of Vailsburg High School. He was also my sister's math teacher. She was a regular mathmagician and I had to frequently remind him that, yes, we are related.

We shared a book and her class was one period after mine. She sat next to the teacher's desk and frequently showed him the notes and doodles I made in his class when I should have been paying attention.

My major problem with math (aside from the inclusion of the alphabet) is that you have to work hard at it. And, you have to check your work. There are no shortcuts and even though you've learned something, you can't skip over it when it shows up in a different problem. There are steps in solving math problems that I don't have the patience to take. I also feel intimidated which affects my performance.

Despite my issues with math, I've been fairly successful in life. *Believe it or not, Mr. Tonero, I don't use algebra in my daily life.*

I'm trying to teach my daughter to avoid the math mistakes that I made the first time I was in the fourth grade. I want her to have good, strong skills now that will help her when Algebra rears its ugly head.

Teens can succeed

We tend to forget how fantastic teenagers can be. We live in a country where teenagers are generally undervalued. We look at them with distaste, distrust and disdain. We put the worst stereotypes on our teenagers especially if they are poor and minority. We expect little good from them. When they falter or fail, we judge them with the moral superiority of the 'older and wiser.'

Our opinions of teens are substantiated by the media that feeds us saggy-bottomed, pink-haired, foul-mouthed, under-achieving losers as poster children for the next generation. We lap up that stereotype because it is easy to swallow.

Teens, if given the opportunity, will spend their middle years working toward college degrees, serving as city mayors and saving county monuments, and they have. If given the opportunity, they will excel at academic decathlons, homecoming games and whatever they set their minds to. They can live up to life's challenges. We've seen plenty of them prove us wrong.

Teenagers don't get near enough recognition for what they do. They seldom make the news and don't stand out in crowds. They spend most of their middle years living down the stereotypes. It can be exhausting, but many of them do succeed.

Here's to all the teens that break the mold!

What's in a name?

My name is Adrian, but I'll answer to Andrea, Andrian or Mr. Jackson. I'll occasionally answer to any variation of my sisters' names: Sandra, Chrishele or Chris, LeAndrea or LeAnn or Lea. I'll answer to Ms. Jackson, if you're nasty.

In a country where kids are saddled with names like Nyguen, Lortensia and Hamsakumari, Adrian should be relatively easy to pronounce. Yet, I find that people mumble and stumble over my name all the time. Are they even trying?

It used to aggravate me, but I've since learned that in the bigger scheme of things, it doesn't matter as long as I get what I want.

There should be some thought put into naming a child. I originally wanted to name my daughter Ariel, but that is the name of laundry detergent in Germany (where we lived when she was born), so I thought better of it. I named her Abrianne. I didn't realize that she would be plagued with mispronunciations for the rest of her life. It's ah-bree-ah-na, not the 150 variations we've heard since she was born.

My daughter's middle names come from my mother and aunt. I think names should mean something and to name a child after a family member is a high honor, in my opinion.

A good friend of mine wanted to name her daughter Florcha. Well, we vetoed that goofy name. She later settled on Jamie and Jemma for her girls. Those two really dodged a bullet.

And what about those magnanimous names that kids have to live up to? An old classmate named her daughter Dominique Devereaux. That's the name of Diane Carroll's character on Dynasty. How is that kid ever to fit in with that name? My daughter had a classmate named D'Artagnan. In case you don't know, this is the name of one of the three musketeers. Are you kidding me? Why not just name the kid, 'kick me'? And then there is Jesus. Do you really want your kid to have to live up to those expectations?

I think kids have to be named with an end goal in mind. If you name a child Billy Lee Ray, Wilbur, Kadeem or Ja'cquon, there is a good chance he may wind up in prison. Or, at the very least, you'll probably not see his name in a law review. On girls' names, I think it is a good idea to avoid alcoholic beverages. Chardonnay, Tanqueray, Zima and Alizé don't go on to graduate from Princeton. Some don't even graduate from high school.

Soccer: A proving ground

The sky was overcast. Two teams faced each other for the second time in the season. You could say they were rivals. Both came to win.

There was only perfunctory participation by the fans. Then, things heated up. Someone fell. Someone else got hit with the ball. A player crashed into her teammate sending them both to the ground. The fans paid attention to what had quickly become a very exciting game.

The goalie kicked a ball into the face of someone from the other team. It looked like she was going to bleed but she didn't. It was still a pretty bad injury though.

As the game got back underway, the fans got caught up. There were shouts of 'Forward. Forward.' Someone yelled, 'Take the ball.' A fan called, 'Protect your goal.' Then, someone stepped on someone else's hand. She had to be carried off the field. It wasn't serious but it looked like it hurt like hell.

Someone said, 'She got what she deserved. We're getting her back for what happened earlier.'

Um, excuse me? Did that woman say she got what she deserved? Is she for real?

The match was between two girls teams. They were eight- to eleven-year olds. The fans were a motley group of parents with varying degrees of understanding of the game. And, apparently, varying degrees of the understanding of the rules of sportsmanship.

It's parents like her that make us all look bad. It's parents like her that show up on the six o'clock news being dragged away by police. It's parents like her that lose sight of the most important lesson in youth sports – it's only a game.

Yep. That's right. There are no FIFA scouts. There is no ESPN coverage. There are no college recruiters. There is no scoreboard. The whole purpose of youth sports is to give local kids (a) an appreciation of the game, (b) a basic understanding of team sports, (c) an outlet for physical activity, and (d) something fun to do. That's really it.

When our actions as parents run contradictory to the league's goals, whether its soccer, basketball, t-ball, youth sports, high school sports or college sports, we run into all sorts of problems. Namely, kids don't love the game and have no fun. Kids get a poor sense of sportsmanship and lose the higher purpose of team sports.

When we parents forget that, it doesn't matter if you win or lose the game it's how you lost the respect of others that counts.

the pitfalls of spelling & grandma

Now that we have spell-check doo we really knead to no how to spell? Is good spelling a lost art? Does anyone even care?

I've gotten lassie in my ole age and my spelling is not as good as it oozed to bee. I right for a living, so I deepened on spell-check quiet a bit. I edit my own work but it is difficult to catch my own errors even after the third tri. Auto-checker an the read underline that pops up in my word processing pogrom take the stress of off my kneading to know how to spill. Steel, there are a handful of words that I consistently botch up:

tommorrow [tomorrow], neccessarily [necessarily], accomodate [accommodate], atleast [at least], definately [definitely], manuever [maneuver], mischievious [mischievious], occassionally [occasionally], sargeant [sergeant], supercede [supersede] defendent [defendant], governer [governor] and leuitenant [lieutenant]. I can spell antidisestablishmentarianism, but soley [solely] escapes me.

I oozed to be a good speller, but the alder I get, the harder it becomes. I have know explanation as to why that is, accept to say that maybe I am just getting more dumber.

And what about grammar.? It, two, is a lost art. Since my business is words, stringing them together are important to me. I do good with the rules of grandma but I have my pitfalls. My biggest problem is me versus I. Frequently, I get stuck on phrases like 'the cake was for he and me/I,' 'it was given to him and me/I,' or 'she and me/I went to the park.' I no the deferens between its and it's thou I mix them up frequently.

I am working currently on an English degree but I don't know if I'd trust myself to teach it. I think a lot of grammatical errors area a result of not paying attention enough to what one is righting. I think that if we reed our work aloud, we will catch most of the mistakes.

And then, there is colloquialisms, which, honestly, like the plaque, we should avoid. Using colloquialisms is like beating a dead horse anyway. If I had my druthers, I'd rather take a crack at being more original.

And last, but not least there is punctuation! I forget frequently to use question marks. Its knot that I don't no when to use them, its just that buy the thyme I get to the end of the sentence, I forgot that it was a question. I especially don't like it when people use a question mark + an exclamation point?! That is just being sarcastic, in my opinion.

Commas are in the eyes of the beholder, I always say. When, and where, and how often, to use comers is really best left up to the righter. Even the best righters wouldn't touch that issue with a ten-foot poll. You could argue for days on this, couldn't you?!

I don't like the use of the ampersand, too. I think that you should use 'and' if that is what you mean. Unless, you are designing a logo, or something! Then, & is O.K.

Life's like a box of Mockolates??!

Have you noticed that there are more candy bars and fewer chocolate bars on store shelves these days? That is because the FDA told chocolatiers that if it has none of the ingredients of chocolate it can't be called chocolate.

The controversy brewed about two years ago when it became common knowledge that some manufacturers replaced the ingredient cocoa butter, essential to chocolate, with vegetable oil. Representatives of Big Chocolate said that in a blind taste test only half of consumers could tell the difference, plus, manufacturers of cheap candies have been using vegetable oil for years.

I'm not a fan of chocolate (un-American, I know) but there is something sinister about this mélange. If today's chocolate bars were grasped out of the air by little Berliners they might be tempted to throw them back at the planes. Chocolate-filled silver platters on royal tables today might offer the delectability of a chicken nugget. Vegetable oil? Really?

Big Chocolate said it is an issue of cost. Let's face it. Vegetable oil is cheaper. If Big Chocoate can convince consumers that they are buying the same chocolate bars they ate as kids, manufacturers can continue to make billions. So what if quality suffers?

The government fought back by clarifying what is and isn't allowed to be called chocolate. If the package says 'milk chocolate,' 'semi-sweet chocolate' or 'bittersweet chocolate' it is real chocolate. If it says 'chocolate flavor,' 'chocolate coating,' 'chocolaty,' or 'made with chocolate' it is the evil twin Mockolate.

I have to give props to the TV series "Friends" where the term 'Mockolate' was introduced during Season 2. Monica 'I have no morals and I need the cash' Geller is hired by a food substitute manufacturer to create Thanksgiving recipes using their fake chocolate.

While the chocolate industry in the U.S. is losing ground with cheap ingredients and slightly pornographic advertising (have you seen Ms. Green M&M?) European manufacturers are flaunting their decadence. Sometimes the percentage of chocolate is printed on the front of the wrapper. You want something milky, go for a 70% bar. You want something dark, go for a 90% bar. You understand that you'll pay more for the higher chocolate content but you don't mind. There is and always will be a level of prestige associated with the consumption of chocolate. After all, for hundreds of years, before the invention of milk chocolate, it was consumed only by the wealthiest consumers.

I have a friend who is a chocolate connoisseur. She gets Godiva chocolates for special occasions. She gets chocolate gift baskets and special collections for birthdays, anniversaries and holidays. She can spot a fake before it ever reaches her lips. Obviously, nobody included her in the taste test.

We need to reclaim our chocolate. Well, I don't. It's not my fight. But if you love chocolate and believe that it should never be sabotaged by the inclusion of vegetable oil, contact your chocolate manufacturer or your Congressman or anyone who will listen and above all else, read the labels and refuse to buy Mockolate. There is power in the purse and if you are willing to pay more for quality you can believe that Big Chocolate will take notice.

Adrian Jackson is a freelance writer in Beeville, Texas and occasionally enjoys a bit of white chocolate. She ate a lavender white chocolate bar recently while in Europe and has somehow been changed by the experience. Yummm!

Just say 'thank you'

A friend complimented me on my column. My response was, 'You know, eventually people are going to start telling me they hate my column.' Inside my head I was thinking, 'Stop talking, stupid! Just say 'thank you.''

Someone complimented me on my hair the other day. My response to her was, 'Oh, this is just a fluke. Most days it looks like a train wreck.' Inside my head I was thinking, 'Stop talking, stupid! Just say 'thank you.'' Why can't I just say thank you?

We are raised in a Puritanical society. We are taught to be humble but with practice we become self-deprecating. We learn to not only deflect compliments, but to diminish them then turn them inside out and make them negative. How did we get this way? Why, when faced with a genuine compliment, do we throw up deflector shields?

In my rational mind I'm appreciative of compliments. There is an underlying level of humility and kindness in giving a compliment. The other person is saying that I am in some way special. That is a gift even if it only lasts a moment.

In my rational mind I'm deserving of compliments. I groom myself daily. I put some thought into my appearance before I leave the house. I'm an interesting person. I'm no conversationalist but I've got some good stories.

In my self-deprecating, irrational mind I'm unworthy of compliments. There are others out there who are nicer, smarter, prettier, blah, blah, blah, than me. But rationally, there are enough compliments for everybody. Is it wrong to accept my share?

In my self-deprecating, irrational mind there's comedy in poking fun at myself. People respond to comedy. It reminds them that I am only human and subject to imperfection, error or outright stupidity. Honesty, they already knew that, so why do I feel I have to restate it? There is humility in comedy. And we really want to get back to the humility because if given a choice between confidence and humility, most of us would take the latter. *This we get from the Puritans.* But there's a short step from humility to self-deprecation and most of us blur the line that we should not cross. Over time, deflecting compliments become de rigueur. So, now that I've devalued myself to the point of being the butt of my own jokes, I've got some improvements to make. We all do. We deserve better. The first step is to learn to just say thank you.

It's time to make upgrades

There comes a point in every woman's life when you realize this is what you've got to work with. At that point, you've got some decisions to make.

On self-image: If you have reached 35 and you still can't look at yourself in the mirror and love the one you're with, you've got to deal with that. No amount of fixing, primping or reconstructing is going to change your basic structure and if you have yet to find the beauty on the inside, it will never, ever radiate to the outside. Once you've accepted your basic self and come to the realization that no man will ever, ever drop dead at the sight of you, you can start on upgrades.

On make-up: Someone said you have the face you're born with in your 20s and the face you deserve in your 40s. If you were blessed enough to get through your 20s with little more than lipstick count your lucky stars. But if your face has the consistency of moon rock make-up really is the only answer.

On cosmetic surgery: Lifts, nips and tucks are good decisions for some. If your goal is to improve upon what you've got, go for it. If surgery will improve an area of your body that causes you grief, have at it. If you think cosmetic surgery will correct what is broken on the inside, you are wasting your money.

On mental health: What goes on in your mind is as important as what goes on in your body. You have to feed your mind with books and good conversations. You have to limit junk food like TV and romance novels. You have to accept that you are precious few steps from being completely insane at any given moment. We all are. Deal with it. Whether it means loving your craziness, talking about it or getting help, you owe it to yourself to stay on this side of sane as long as you can.

On physical health: You've accepted your basic self so how does your body fit into that? You can accept your body as it is or you can change it. You can stop thinking about your body every ten seconds of every day. Do something or make a firm decision to do nothing.

On well-being: You know who you are. You love yourself. You accept your gifts and limitations. Now, decide what you can live with and what's got to go. Surround yourself with the things and people that bring you joy. Decide what you can live without and do without it. Develop a relationship with a doctor you can trust and follow his or her guidelines to achieving a healthy lifestyle.

On love: Joy, happiness and love have positive impacts on your body. You can never have enough of the stuff. Seek love, accept love, give love and exude love.

On goals: Decide what you are good at and do that. You don't have to do everything or be involved in everything or even be relied upon for everything. Be that person people come to for one thing. Be the one-who-makes-great-cakes or the good listener or the person-who-can-get-things-done.

On time: Make choices about where your time is best spent. Don't let other people impinge on your precious time. Stay only if you want to. Participate only if you truly have the time to give. Don't sacrifice the time you spend on something you love for something you feel obligated to do.

May God grant you the strength to accept what you can't change and upgrade where you can.

Made in the USA
Lexington, KY
04 August 2010